SCHOOLING FOR
THE NEW SLAVERY

DONALD SPIVEY

SCHOOLING FOR THE NEW SLAVERY

Black Industrial Education, 1868-1915

Contributions in Afro-American and African Studies, Number 38

GREENWOOD PRESS
WESTPORT, CONNECTICUT • LONDON, ENGLAND

Library of Congress Cataloging in Publication Data

Spivey, Donald.
  Schooling for the new slavery.

  (Contributions in Afro-American and African studies ;
no. 38 ISSN 0069-9624)
  Bibliography: p.
  Includes index.
  1. Afro-Americans—Education—United States—
History. 2. Manual training—United States—History.
I. Title. II. Series.
LC2801.S65   371.9'7'96073   77-87974
ISBN 0-313-20051-3

Library of Congress Catalog Card Number: 77-87974
ISBN: 0-313-20051-3
ISSN: 0069-9624

First published in 1978

Greenwood Press, Inc.
51 Riverside Avenue, Westport, Connecticut 06880

Printed in the United States of America

10 9 8 7 6 5 4 3 2 1

It may be of no importance to the race to be able to boast today of many times as many "educated" members as it had in 1865. If they are of the wrong kind the increase in numbers will be a disadvantage rather than an advantage. The only question which concerns us here is whether these "educated" persons are actually equipped to face the ordeal before them or unconsciously contribute to their own undoing by perpetuating the regime of the oppressor.

—Carter G. Woodson,
The Mis-education of the Negro (1933)

CONTENTS

PREFACE

Blacks faced a neo-slave system when the Civil War ended. Cotton still had to be picked, tobacco fields needed to be tended, and menial labor was required for the industries of the New South. It has been documented that sharecropping, debt peonage, and convict lease were means used to resubjugate black labor and that the South sought through jim crow, night riders, and lynch law to nullify the civil and political rights guaranteed to blacks under the Thirteenth, Fourteenth, and Fifteenth amendments. But another tool was also used against blacks: industrial education.

Scholarly studies on the New South have been numerous and have increased our knowledge of America's history. But our understanding of the role of industrial schooling has only slightly advanced beyond the criticism launched against it by W.E.B. Du Bois at the beginning of the century. Even the more recent histories of education in the South have focused primarily on questions of educational opportunity and segregation rather than on industrial schooling, its complexities, and its goals.

Industrial education was a major force in the subjugation of black labor in the New South. This study focuses on the *whys* of that schooling, with special attention to race relations, the interests of Northern industrialists, and leadership within the African-American community. In addition, the cultural aspect and international impact of industrial education are explored. Conceptually, my theme stems from the basic premise that the history of black people in America is primarily a labor history. The Africans were, after all, brought to this country for their labor. The death of the formal institution of slavery did not abolish that relationship.

Samuel Chapman Armstrong, the founder of Hampton Institute and ideological father of black industrial education, tried to solve the race problem through education. He believed that blacks should be taught to remain in their place, stay out of politics, keep quiet about their rights, and work. The educational theme that he emphasized was the need for blacks to be good, subservient laborers.

Thus, the reader should not have to conjure up an elaborate conspiracy theory to understand why industrial education received full support from Northern industrialists who had economic interests in the South. Nor should it be difficult to believe that the industrial schooling idea was applicable beyond the Southern states.

ACKNOWLEDGMENTS

This study benefited from the careful readings, perceptive criticisms, and suggestions of many individuals, none of whom are directly responsible for the methods employed and conclusions reached. My deepest debt is to David Brody for his wise counsel. I am extremely grateful to Daniel H. Calhoun and C. Roland Marchand for fruitful comments and perspicacious suggestions, to Wilson Smith for some early advice, and to Frederic Cople Jaher for crucial guidance at the initial stage of my work. I am also indebted to Ifoma Baratunde, Robert O'dell, Harvey Schwartz, Mark Farber, James Anderson, and Eugene Elk. They graciously listened to my thoughts and shared many ideas.

In my research I received numerous courtesies from the library staffs of the following institutions: Library of Congress; Williams College, especially Sarah McFarland, research librarian; Hampton Institute; Rockefeller Archives, Tarreytown, New York; University of Illinois; University of Chicago; National Archives; Harvard University; Fisk University; Dillard University; Syracuse University; Tuskegee Institute; University of Michigan; University of California at Los Angeles, and Berkeley. I owe a special note of appreciation to the timely assistance of the Inter-library Loan Department of the University of California at Davis, Gladys Taylor and Carolyn Crowell in particular. Through their persistent effort they procured the infinite number of micro-films and books that I requested and thereby saved me addition-al time and travel. My sincere thanks to the Graduate Research Committee of the University of California at Davis for award-ing me the Patent Fund Research Grant in 1973 and an Inter-campus Research Grant in 1976.

My wife, Diane, served as typist, proofreader, and historical critic. They are only some of the reasons why this book is dedicated to her.

SCHOOLING FOR THE NEW SLAVERY

1

THE MAKING OF FREE SLAVES

A Prelude

*What is needed here
is an education of
the head, hand, and
heart.*

—Samuel Chapman Armstrong (1868)

The widespread belief that the newly emancipated slaves were a childlike people, inferior and unable to fend for themselves, existed in the white North and South after the Civil War ended. An outgrowth of that belief was that the Freedmen's Bureau was established to aid and protect the freedmen. This sympathetic interpretation, however, overlooks the role of the Bureau as a conservative bulwark against black self-assertion. As the dominant authority over black destinies at the end of the Civil War, the Bureau clearly indicated with its actions that the newly found black freedom was to be severely circumscribed. Northerners who directed the organization, such as Samuel Chapman Armstrong, who was in charge in Hampton, Virginia, were more concerned with bringing order and stability to the South than with helping to uplift the blacks.

Freedmen were extremely discontented with restraints placed upon them. They were eager to become their own masters and to elevate themselves from their traditional position as prostrate laborers. They believed that freedom meant, among other things, self-rule and self-reliance, and they asserted themselves toward these ends. The result was that they often found themselves at odds with the Bureau as well as with the hostile South. This was as true of the Freedmen's Bureau under the authority of Samuel Chapman Armstrong in Hampton as it was elsewhere in the South.

Hampton blacks became wildly elated when Northern troops took charge of the area in 1862. There were approximately three thousand blacks in Hampton, but the number increased with the daily arrival of hundreds of fleeing slaves seeking sanctuary behind Union lines. Both the resident and newly arrived contraband, as the blacks were often called, learned quickly, however, to fear the "Blue Bellie" almost as much as they feared the slave-master. On numerous occasions Union troopers attacked and raped black women, debased black dwellings, and stole food from the freedmen. One witness characterized the soldiers' actions as being "beyond redemption."[1] Crops and livestock were confiscated. Freedmen labor colonies were established. Able-bodied black men and women were conscripted into service as forced laborers under Union overseers.[2] Other blacks, desirous to fight "on the side of freedom," willingly served the Union forces at Hampton in whatever capacity they could. The military promised a fair wage to both reluctant and willing blacks laboring in its service—eight dollars a month for men and four for women. The wages never materialized, however. Instead, as set forth in General Wool's Directive of 14 October 1861, payment to blacks was made in clothing and the remaining money placed in a fund for those blacks unable to work. In actuality, blacks received little or nothing; unscrupulous quartermasters made a tidy profit.[3]

Blacks were accustomed to the mistreatment of slavery, but they had expected better from Northerners. Fearful that their treatment by the Union army might be a preview of life after the war, some Hampton freedmen seriously contemplated exodus to Haiti. John Lockwood, a Hampton missionary, reported that because of the attitude of the Union military, many blacks feared that even if the North won the war, they would be reenslaved.[4]

Although Hampton blacks began to sense their grim future in America, they found in the actions of a few Northern whites reason to be optimistic. An organization they viewed most favorably was the Bureau of Negro Affairs and particularly its superintendent for the area, Charles B. Wilder. Responsible for the Bureau's activities throughout the entire Fortress Monroe, Hampton, Virginia region from 1863 to 1865, Wilder worked in earnest to aid the refugee and resident blacks. Though the Bureau was technically controlled by the military, Wilder lashed out at the way the Union troops treated the freedmen. He actively sought an end to injustices. Moreover, he believed that blacks should be given a share in America's wealth. In many respects C. B. Wilder was a true firebrand in the best tradition of Thaddeus Stevens and Charles Sumner. He advocated that abandoned rebel plantations be divided among the freedmen. Wilder argued that freedom alone was not enough and that the North must also contribute to the long-range survival of the former slaves. This could be done, he and other sympathizers believed, by giving the freedmen land. Land redistribution became a general practice in the region under Wilder's authority. Blacks in his district eagerly worked on land that was, at least for the moment, their own. Farms sprouted and plantations seemed to blossom overnight. By 1864 black Hampton had taken on the appearance of a community in the making.[5]

But when the Civil War ended, many of the gains were lost.[6] The Bureau of Negro Affairs was soon replaced with the more conservative Bureau of Abandoned Lands and Refugees—the Freedmen's Bureau. The desire for reconciliation between North and South characterized Lincoln-Johnson Reconstruction, the so-called Radical Reconstruction period, and Freedmen Bureau policy. Reconciliation signaled the return of confiscated lands to their previous owners. Blacks were uprooted in spite of every effort they made to keep the land. Cases of land reclamation were brought before the civil and Freedmen Bureau courts, but the verdict rendered nearly always supported the rebel.

Conflicts were bound to occur because exconfederates not only wanted their land back but also sought to reestablish many of the idiosyncrasies of the Old South. After "de Massa" regained partial hold of some of his former power, he made an offer to blacks—an offer they could hardly refuse. He offered them an alternative to remaining wards of the federal government. He would provide shelter and food; the blacks would repay him with their labor, of course. Hampton's freedmen population recognized that there was only a small difference between tenant farming and chattel slavery and practically no difference between slavery and sharecropping; but submission to this systematic exploitation proved to be unavoidable. The Old-South way of doing things in many respects became operative once again. One embittered Hampton black complained that in addition to being forced to return the land to and go to work for former slave-masters, "the rebels require the same manners now as in slavery, we must say 'Master' and 'Mistress.'"[7]

Wilder, who had been appointed the first superintendent of the Freedmen's Bureau in Hampton, sided with the blacks in their complaints and paid for it. He desired a more punitive reconstruction policy for the South. Nevertheless, when the time came for blacks to actually give up the land and many refused to do so, Wilder was charged with removing them. He adhered to the orders for removal, but only in the most reluctant fashion. Hampton freedmen were being returned to their traditional role in the South as workers of the land rather than as landowners. With the land taken from them, they were forced to accept employment under their former employer, de Massa himself, and often on the same land that had momentarily belonged to them. Given the white landlords' willingness to defraud their black laborers, the working relationship between the two was unstable and ripe with conflicts. Blacks complained to Wilder about how they were being treated, and on numerous occasions they refused to work. Wilder championed the blacks' cause and as a result placed his life in jeopardy. An unsuccessful attempt was made to assassinate him.[8] The white landlords were so upset by his sympathetic attitude toward the freedmen that they complained constantly about him to the Bureau's national headquarters. General Oliver Otis Howard, national head of the Freedmen's Bureau, decided to have Wilder replaced.[9] In his study of O. O. Howard and the freedmen, McFeely concluded: "Bureau men Howard removed from the South were considered undesirable and unfit, not because of laziness or dishonesty, but because when they tried to help the freedmen, powerful white men complained."[10]

A strong supporter of Bureau philosophy and policy, General Samuel Chapman Armstrong was the perfect replacement for Wilder. Officers in charge of the Freedmen's Bureau had the utmost confidence in Armstrong's ability and believed he could be counted on to bring order to Hampton. Order meant halting any further black self-assertion, which had plagued Wilder's stay in office. The unsettled condition between blacks and whites in the Hampton district made the position there of Freedmen's Bureau Superintendent, in Howard's words, "the most delicate post in the Bureau."[11] Two concerns occupied Bureau officials: the problems connected with the restoration of land to former confederate owners and the sporadic labor condition in the area brought on by freedmen discontent.

Armstrong carried out his orders quickly and in good conscience. He supervised the return of lands to their former rebel owners in Hampton. Under his direction, "as fast as practicable these [lands] were restored to the former owners—or their heirs —unless some public need demanded their appraisal and purchase, or sale, by Government."[12] He did, however, indicate a tinge of remorse in seeing the blacks left landless, but at the same time he saw their plight as best for them:

> Most of the land was given back to the owners by Government, under our direction. It was hard on the colored people often. I was sorry for them and would have liked sometimes to do differently. Yet I believe it was on the whole better for them. It put them at the bottom of the ladder. . . . It is not a bad thing for any one to touch bottom early, if there is a good solid foundation under him and then climb from that.[13]

It is difficult to recognize the solid foundation from which the freedmen were supposed to climb, since one, if not the most basic, of all ingredients for sustenance and elevation—land—was systematically denied them. Armstrong's sympathies, however, lay in achieving "a settled order of things" in Hampton.

He moved swiftly toward establishing a legalized and stabilized black-white work relationship in the area. Armstrong instigated contracts as the means to bringing greater stability to labor relations in Hampton. As Armstrong reported it, the concern was that "whites say 'niggers won't work'; negroes say 'whites won't pay.' " He believed that if you "furnish capital and confidence," there "will be no troubles about labor."[14]

Capital and confidence, however, are no guarantee for equity and justice. All that Armstrong gave the blacks was weak sympathy. "The freed people," he confided to his mother, "are crushed by high rents, often from one quarter to one half the value of the land and houses they occupy—most have to put their children out to service to their employers to make up rent." He recognized this condition for what it was, "a species of slavery for both the parents and children putting them completely in the power of white men." He added: "The colored people . . . feel keenly their condition, hope for nothing from their employers and were it not for the suffrage would be practically slaves."[15] Armstrong did not mention that the notorious Black Codes continued to flourish in Hampton well after 1866. Moreover, in spite of his seemingly sympathetic revelations, he made no connection between the predicament of the blacks and his role with the Bureau in the failure to constructively aid the cause of black freedom. Rather, he attributed much of the blame for the freedmen's condition on the freedmen themselves.

He contended that the real problem was the laziness of the blacks. "Freedmen as a class," General Armstrong declared, "are destitute of ambition; their complacency in poverty and filth is a curse; discontent would lead to determined effort and a better life."[16] And in their most important function as laborers, he believed that the majority of them were worthless: "One third are eye servants [workers that will only perform under the watchful eye of a white supervisor], and worth little or nothing; of the remainder, only another third could really be considered good workmen." He stated that the freedmen's entire life-style demonstrated their lack of resourcefulness: "They have no aspirations, or healthy ambitions; everything about them, their clothes, their houses, *their lands* [italics mine], their fences all bear witness to their shiftless propensity."[17]

In light of General Samuel Chapman Armstrong's view of blacks, it is indeed understandable that he often found it extremely difficult to maintain the favor and trust of the freedmen population.[18] Ironic as it may seem, Armstrong considered himself to be one of the best friends of the freedmen.[19] He was, in fact, a better friend to Southern men of property. After all, as he saw it, the best class of Southern whites, "men of property," would work to bring order and stability to Hampton and throughout the South.[20]

What concerned Armstrong and the Bureau most was the need for order and economic stabilization. This is clear from his talk of the need for "moral influences" to be more greatly applied upon Hampton blacks. For the blacks, the General said, "moral influences must be brought to bear; payment of rents be vigorously enforced and all duties as citizens be required, idleness prevented."[21] The idleness he spoke of was the blacks' occasional refusal to work or very half-hearted manner of working in their continued effort to challenge their exploitative white landlords. Armstrong talked about precepts under which only blacks were expected to abide. Nothing was done to check the landowners in their exploitation of black tenants. The lyrics of "moral influences" that Armstrong sung were set in harmony to the tune of the prevailing race-caste status quo of Anglo-Saxon rule and black subordination to it, which existed in Hampton and throughout the South as well as in the North.

What Armstrong wanted to achieve was "a settled order of things; no humanity could be greater than to hasten the adoption of a final organic law that should establish fixed relations which are basic to all economical operations."[22] On justice and equity—to say nothing of equality—the General was silent. And for those freedmen who could not or would not adapt to the final organic law that Armstrong professed, he suggested that they be made to leave the area. If necessary, the General said,

"I believe in scattering the people [blacks]. . . . Emigration to Florida may yet in a measure succeed: it should be wisely urged."[23]

Despite the threat—or blessing—of banishment, blacks continued to assert themselves against injustices in Hampton. They sought within the Freedmen Courts of the Freedmen's Bureau to challenge the exploitative white landlords. The judges sitting at the head of the Freedmen Courts were, in many instances, some of the very same men who had faced the rebel "Gray Coats" bayonet-to-bayonet on the battlefield. However, the courts rarely showed partiality for black over gray.

The continued agitation for justice by blacks in the courts had the effect of heightening the sensitivities of the Bureau and Armstrong. It was finally deemed necessary to compromise the situation. After some deliberation, General Armstrong decided in May 1866 that the blacks be represented on the Freedmen Courts. The freedmen were jubilant. They called a meeting and elected one of their black brethren to represent them on the courts. To their dismay, this was rejected by Armstrong. His notion of giving blacks representation was to appoint a "sympathetic" white man to represent blacks.[24]

Dejected and outraged, yet powerless, freedmen began to secure for themselves the type of power that the rebels, the Freedmen's Bureau, and anyone else would be sure to understand. Fights and shootings occurred on several occasions between die-hard rebels and freedmen. Increasing numbers of freedmen armed themselves and were, as one Bureau officer put it, "ready" and "willing" to take on all comers. It was brought to Armstrong's attention that an armed militant black organization was being formed to "defend blacks against both the rebels and the Bureau."[25]

If a good fight was what they were looking for, General Armstrong was willing to oblige. He was a strict authoritarian who believed in the sanctity of authority, especially when he thought it was his authority being questioned. He also believed in fighting fire with fire. Armstrong authorized Bureau personnel to use whatever force was necessary to thwart any armed aggression against Bureau authority.[26] The situation in Hampton seemed ripe for a major confrontation between the freedmen and the Bureau, but the showdown never came. Samuel Chapman Armstrong kept the lid secure on the bubbling caldron of black discontent with armed patrols and search and seizure.

If the Bureau's mission was to advance black freedom, it certainly failed drastically. Freedom was never a reality for blacks under Armstrong and the Bureau in Hampton, Virginia. The Freedmen's Bureau was successful, however, in the sense that, as W.E.B. Du Bois noted, it "set going a system of free labor." In actuality, tenant farming, sharecropping, and debt peonage are terms that more aptly describe the type of "free labor" that was nurtured under Bureau auspices in Hampton, Virginia. When Du Bois credited the Bureau with "the recognition of black free men before courts of law," he was correct. They did receive recognition before the courts; justice they did not. Du Bois was accurate, however, when he noted that the Bureau provided education for the black South.[27] There would be no greater champion to the cause of Southern black education than Samuel Chapman Armstrong. But what sort of education would Armstrong deem proper for the South's black population?

By the end of 1867 Armstrong had moved into the educational arena. The General had arrived at the opinion that the freedmen presented a problem that could only be solved through proper schooling. The "only thing is to educate them [blacks]," he declared; "there is no other escape from a fearful band of evils that their ignorance will otherwise entail upon the country."[28] The problem, as he saw it, for his district and for the entire South was the continued unstable condition of race and labor relations. It is understandable to a degree that he would turn to the schoolhouse for the final solution to the problem. The son of parents who had been educational missionaries in Hawaii, Armstrong had a lingering salvationist faith in the power of proper schooling and an unquenched missionary desire to some day be a leading figure in the education of the "uncivilized." In 1868 Samuel Chapman Armstrong, with the assistance of the Freedmen's Bureau and the American

Missionary Association, founded the Hampton Normal Institute in Hampton, Virginia, an institute that would embody his ideas of education for blacks.

NOTES

1. John Oliver to American Missionary Association, 5 August 1862, *American Missionary Association Collection*, Fisk University (now at Dillard University).

2. Traditionally, studies have pointed to the conscription of black labor by the Confederates. See, for example, James H. Brewer, *The Confederate Negro: Virginia's Craftsmen and Military Laborers, 1861-1865* (Durham, N.C.: Duke University Press, 1969), especially Chapter 1, "Negro Mobilization: Impressment Laws and Voluntary Hiring-Out," pp. 3-16, and Chapter 6, "Confederate Labor Troops," pp. 131-164.

Numerous laws were enacted by the Confederacy for the impressment of black laborers. See, for example, June Purcell Guild, *Black Laws of Virginia: A Summary of the Legislative Acts of Virginia Concerning Negroes from Earliest Times to the Present* (New York: Negro University Press, 1936), p. 195 and passim.

Freedmen labor was widely exploited during Reconstruction:

> The compensation offered the freedmen, however, was not generally attractive. The farmers had preconceived notions that free Negro labor would be inefficient, and they believed that the freedmen would not work without compulsion. Therefore, the farmers determined to settle the question of wages without reference to the needs of the Negroes, and without soliciting their opinion on the worth of their labor. The farmers held that they were impoverished and could not pay high wages. Most of them decided that five dollars a month should constitute the wages of an ablebodied male laborer, but the pay to women and boys should be smaller. They agreed not to employ a Negro who could not obtain the recommendation of his former master. . . .
>
> The repressive labor combination exerted a disastrous effect upon the freedmen. Compelled to work for inadequate wages, restricted in their freedom of employment, opposed in their ambition to obtain land in some quarters, the freedmen became disgruntled and restless. [Alrutheus Ambush

Taylor, *The Negro in the Reconstruction of Virginia* (New
York: Russell and Russell Pubs. [1926] 1969), pp. 106,
107.]

Black labor was also exploited by the Union Army, and before Reconstruction. See John Oliver to American Missionary Association, 5 August
1862, *American Missionary Association Collection*, Fisk University; John
Lockwood to American Missionary Association, 7 April 1862, *American
Missionary Association Collection*; Edward L. Pierce, *Enfranchisement
and Citizenship: Addresses and Papers*, ed. A. N. Stevens (Boston: Roberts
Brothers, 1896), pp. 36-50; *Thirty-seventh Congress, 2nd Session, House
of Representatives, Executive Document No. 85*, "Africans in Fort Monroe
Military District: A Letter from the Secretary of War" (Washington, D.C.,
1863). "States still in rebellion were divided into five districts, each with
its special agent for freedmen, and certain tracts in each district were set
apart as 'Freedmen's Labor Colonies.' " [Francis Greenwood Peabody,
Education for Life: The Story of Hampton Institute (New York: Doubleday, Page and Company, 1918), p. 41; P. G. Pierce, "The Freedmen's
Bureau," *Bulletin of State University of Iowa* 74 (1904), p. 24.]

3. *Thirty-seventh Congress, 2nd Session, House of Representatives
Executive Document No. 85*, "Africans in Fort Monroe Military District:
A Letter from the Secretary of War" (Washington, D.C., 1863), p. 2.

4. John Lockwood to American Missionary Association, 7 April 1862,
American Missionary Association Collection.

5. Edward K. Graham's manuscript, "A Tender Violence: The Biography of a College," Chapter 1. Graham is Professor emeritus, Hampton
Institute. His manuscript is not only an in-house, uncritical history of
Hampton Institute but a thorough examination of the black community
of Hampton. Graham supports the idea of a black community developing
in Hampton before and after the end of the Civil War. Similar conclusions
are reached using a more critical perspective in Robert Engs's "The Development of Black Culture and Community in the Emancipation Era: Hampton Roads, Virginia, 1861-1870" (Ph.D. Dissertation, Yale University,
1972), pp. 95-98.

6. C. B. Wilder to General Orlando Brown, 18 October 1865 and 18
January 1866, *Records of the Bureau of Refugees, Freedmen, and Abandoned Lands* (hereafter referred to as *Records of the BRF&AL)*, Virginia,
Letters Received, National Archives. Even Samuel Chapman Armstrong
alluded to what he thought was a worsened condition for black Hamp-
tonians with the end of the Civil War. Samuel Chapman Armstrong to
General Orlando Brown, "Quarterly Report," 30 June 1866, *Records of
the BRF&AL*, Virginia, Letters Received.

7. Quoted in Samuel Chapman Armstrong to General Orlando Brown, 30 June 1866, *Records of the BRF&AL*, Virginia, Letters Received. A second copy of this letter is also available in the *Samuel Chapman Armstrong Collection*, Hampton Institute.

8. Lt. Massey to Samuel Chapman Armstrong, 23 May 1866, *Records of the BRF&AL*, Virginia, Letters Received.

9. Samuel Chapman Armstrong to Mrs. Clarissa Chapman Armstrong, 14 November 1866, *Armstrong Family Papers*, Williams College.

10. William S. McFeely, *Yankee Stepfather: General O. O. Howard and the Freedmen* (New York: W. W. Norton and Company, 1970), p. 5.

11. Samuel Chapman Armstrong to Mrs. Clarissa Armstrong, 14 November 1866, *Armstrong Family Papers*.

12. *Ludlow Collection*, Hampton Institute and Williams College. Helen Ludlow, ed., *Personal Memoirs and Letters of General Samuel Chapman Armstrong: Hawaii, Williams, War, Hampton* (3: 1894), p. 590. This is part of a multi-volume collection (1,408 pages) that is a fund of valuable Armstrong letters. The letters, however, are often undated and without a heading.

13. Ibid., p. 515.

14. Ibid., p. 556.

15. Samuel Chapman Armstrong to Mrs. Clarissa Chapman Armstrong, 30 April 1867, *Ludlow Collection* 3, p. 586.

16. Ibid., p. 555.

17. Samuel Chapman Armstrong to General Orlando Brown, "Quarterly Report," 30 June 1868, *Records of the BRF&AL*, Virginia, Letters Received.

18. Samuel Chapman Armstrong to Yardley Warner, 1 March 1867, *Samuel Chapman Armstrong Collection*, Hampton Institute.

19. Samuel Chapman Armstrong to General Orlando Brown, 6 June 1866, *Records of the BRF&AL*, Virginia, Letters Received.

20. Samuel Chapman Armstrong to Mrs. Clarissa Chapman Armstrong, 15 March 1867, *Armstrong Family Papers*.

21. Letter by Samuel Chapman Armstrong, *Ludlow Collection* 3, p. 550.

22. Samuel Chapman Armstrong to General Orlando Brown, 26 March 1867, *Records of the BRF&AL*, Virginia, Letters Received.

23. Letter by Samuel Chapman Armstrong, *Ludlow Collection* 3, p. 554.

24. Samuel Chapman Armstrong to Lt. Massey, 15 May 1866, *Records of the BRF&AL*, Virginia, Letters Received.

25. Lt. Massey to Samuel Chapman Armstrong, 16 May 1866, *Records of the BRF&AL*, Virginia, Letters Received. The Hampton organization

and the Black Panther Party of the late 1960s were both founded on a principle of self-defense. The Hampton organization, like the early Panthers, was well armed.

26. Samuel Chapman Armstrong to Lt. Massey, 20 May 1866, *Records of the BRF&AL*, Virginia, Letters Received.

27. W.E.B. Du Bois, "The Freedmen's Bureau," *Atlantic Monthly* 87 (March 1901), p. 363.

28. Samuel Chapman Armstrong to Mrs. Clarissa Armstrong, 15 March 1867, *Armstrong Family Papers.*

2

SCHOOLING FOR THE NEW SLAVERY: THE INDUSTRIAL EDUCATION MODEL, 1868-93

The training of the schools we need to-day more than ever—the training of deft hands, quick eyes and ears, and above all, the broader, deeper, higher culture of gifted minds and pure hearts. The power of the ballot we need in sheer self-defence,—else what shall save us from a second slavery?

—W.E.B. Du Bois,
The Souls of Black Folk (1903)

Slavery's stabilizing influence was gone. The Civil War let loose upon the South millions of freedom-seeking blacks. What to do with them was the severest issue facing the new nation. Suggestions ranged from shipping all blacks back to Africa, to making them immediate and full citizens, to leaving them to the tender mercies of the South. The Freedmen's Bureau served as a tentative and at best temporary remedy. But in Hampton, Virginia, Samuel Chapman Armstrong, Freedmen's Bureau superintendent, initiated his own solution to the "Negro problem." He proposed to educate blacks with a special kind of schooling, one that would advance reconciliation between North and South and at the same time secure in the southland lasting peace and order between the races. In short, he planned to imbue the freedmen with those characteristics befitting the "Negro's place." This brand of education for blacks eventually swept across the Southern states. In a sense, the schoolhouse was to replace the stability lost by the demise of the institution of slavery.

Armstrong believed that in the training and dissemination of black teachers throughout the black communities of the South lay the solution to the race problem. At Hampton he advocated "the production of wise leaders, of peacemakers, rather than noisy and dangerous demagogues."[1] These teachers, these future black leaders, were to be functionaries, subordinate to white leadership. This conformed to the General's belief that the Negro was incapable of self-rule. "The colored race has," he contended, "never, except in Liberia and Hayti, lived under an organization of its own, and, so far, its efforts from colonies to cooperative stores, have been without marked success."[2] Morover, supporters of Armstrong's position, such as Francis Greenwood Peabody, thought that because "the mind of the Negro is not hampered either by tradition or by self-esteem" and blacks are "impressionable and imitative," they could easily be educated and taught "a habit of restraint." Citing what he termed were demonstrated black characteristics under the peculiar institution, Peabody contended, "Even slaveholders could count on the docility and loyalty of the Negroes under conditions from which other races would have rebelled." He added, in support of Armstrong's proposal, "The same traits, steadied by liberty and guided by affection, make of the Negro students the most plastic material for education."[3]

Samuel Chapman Armstrong argued that the type of education suited for blacks was industrial education. Industrial schooling had originated with European educational theorists in the early nineteenth century and had become part of a worldwide movement for technical and agricultural schools by the 1860s.[4] Armstrong had studied educational theory while a student at Williams College before the Civil War, but his practical indoctrination to industrial education had come years earlier under the tutelage of his father, Richard Armstrong, who had served as Minister of Public Instruction in Hawaii from 1848 to 1860.

Samuel's father and his mother, Clarissa Armstrong, began service in Hawaii in 1843 as educational missionaries. Richard urged a special kind of education for the natives.

> My general plan is to aim at the improvement of the heart, the head and the body at once. This is a lazy people and if they are ever to be made industrious the work must begin with the young. So I am making strenuous efforts to have some sort of manual labour connected with every school. . . .[5]

Steeped in the Puritan Ethic, Richard thought that industrial education was the best way to instill in the Hawaiians the virtues of hard work and Christian morality. Yet he did not speak out against the exploitation of the natives by his fellow missionaries, who were buying up large tracts of land and establishing sugar plantations run on native labor.[6] Nor was Richard egalitarian in his teaching. Native children were taught that they were not as good as whites. The Armstrongs believed in discrimination and segregation between whites and Hawaiians. One indication of this was their fear of the influence that the native children seemed to have on their own children. It upset Clarissa and Richard that their daughter, Caroline, "imitates all they [the natives] do. . . . We hope to keep her from them more, when our house is done and has high walls around it."[7] Richard described the Hawaiians as a licentious people. "[S] warms of native girls," he wrote, "stand ready to gratify any youth, day or night, and are not backward to make advances for that purpose. If a young man is saved, it is 'by fire.' "[8] Clarissa's concern for her children, in addition to her poor health, made her, as Richard reported, "quite inclined to think that we had better return to the United States for good."[9]

Samuel adopted his parents' attitudes. He thought of Hawaiians as "a savage people."[10] He had an even lower opinion of Mexicans and in particular Mexican women, whom he characterized as being "dirty," "nasty-looking," and "smelling worse than brimstone."[11] Blacks, however, in Samuel's estimate had potential over Mexicans and Hawaiians because of their numbers and stamina. "Children are abundant. The pickaninies do not seem destined to die young," he noted. "They are a numerous, frisky, healthy class of unfailing humore and appetite, as unlike as anything can be to the sor-spotted Hawaiian child whose race is doomed."[12]

His decision in 1867 to open a manual labor school for blacks in Hampton came in part from his faith in industrial schooling as a solution to the race problem, his role as Freedmen's Bureau superintendent, and from a class consciousness similar to that of his missionary parents. Like his parents, Samuel thought that "the test of the civilization of any nation is the care it gives its ignorant and oppressed classes."[13] And like his parents he felt obliged to serve humanity but not to fight or challenge oppression. Samuel contended that Hawaiians and blacks were their own worse enemy. "The chief difficulty was," he said, "with them [Hawaiians], deficient character, as it is with the Negro."[14]

His low opinion of blacks went even further. In his list of black character deficiencies Armstrong included "improvidence, low ideas of honor and morality, and a general lack of directive energy, judgment and foresight."[15] He thought it fair to state, by way of classification, that "a large third, say three millions" of the eight million or more "Negroes are a 'low down' shiftless class . . . lazy . . . living from hand to mouth . . . grossly immoral."[16]

At Hampton he would work to alter black character. The school would devote little attention to disciplining blacks in the traditional three R's. "[T]he negro's deficiencies of character," Armstrong said, "are worse for him and for the world than his mere ignorance."[17] The Founder professed that his goal at Hampton Institute was to "civilize" the blacks, to imbue them with "general deportment . . . habits of living and of labor . . . and right ideas of life and duty."[18]

Utmost in the Hampton process of remaking the black was the use of labor as a guiding force. The General maintained that labor was "the greatest moral force in civilization."[19] He advocated that "the training of the hand was at the same time a training of the mind and will."[20] Armstrong believed that, when

properly applied, manual labor schooling provided the highest
likelihood of "civilizing" the black. When it opened in 1868,
Hampton Institute proceeded to develop according to its
founder's philosophy.

Students at Hampton spent most of their time engaged in
menial labor outside of the classroom. This was particularly
true during the first year of attendance. "The new Negro boys,"
the General reported, "work at various kinds of unskilled labor
for one year, going to school two hours in the evening."[21]

Black women were treated in the same way. The Founder
saw no need to discriminate between the sexes. In fact, he
believed it essential to educate both men and women. "The
family is," he remarked, "the unit of civilization, and the conditions of pure family living are the first things to be created
in educating men and women. Hence the co-education of the
sexes is indispensable."[22]

The admission of women to the school dated back to the
very beginning of the institution. From the first days, they
received training in household duties and obtained the majority of their in-class instruction at the Women's Labor Department, which was established in 1868.[23] The school boasted that the young women of the middle and senior class received instruction in the art of bread-making and of plain
cooking, and that all the girls did housework, washing, and ironing throughout their years at Hampton. It was hoped that this
sort of training instilled in them the dignity of labor.[24]

The school's newspaper, the *Southern Workman*, was edited
by Armstrong and echoed his belief in the virtue of labor.
Throughout the pages of the *Workman*, the General reminded
the students, alumni, and public that "what men want is not
talent, it is purpose: in other words, not the power to achieve,
but the will of labor."[25] He advised blacks that if they devoted
themselves to labor, they would grow in character and purpose.
Often the *Southern Workman* carried short work-ethic stories.
One such story titled, "The Boy Who Worked," told of a poor
black boy who worked hard at whatever job he could obtain,
and by this he grew in stature and character: "Thus it was that
the boy who worked came to be a real gentleman at last."[26]

The *Workman* included poems that carried a labor message. One poem focused on the need to be jovial at whatever task was given and concluded with a reminder that "Love Lightens Labor."[27] Often the message in the *Workman* came undiluted. Armstrong told blacks that the formula for bringing greater virtue into their lives was very simple: "Work, work, work."[28]

The General, however, assessed the value of black labor from a far less philosophical and much more profit-oriented perspective. "The Negro," he advised his fellow countrymen, "is important to the country's prosperity."[29] As Armstrong saw it, the black still held "the *empire of labour* [italics mine] which was surrendered to him in slavery."[30] Throughout the pages of the *Southern Workman*, he advocated the full utilization of the South's best natural resource: black labor. The Southern Railway, which blacks had largely constructed, advertised in the *Workman* and endorsed the General's work. The tobacco industry owed its very existence to black labor, which was the dominant source of labor in its fields. The industry supported the General's position.[31] Moreover, as was pointed out in the *Workman*, the movement of machinery into the South would increase the industrial rate of production and, therefore, the demand for labor. Considering all this, Armstrong estimated that there was "no source whatever of a suitable supply in lieu of Negro labor in the South." The black was indispensable to Southern prosperity. "Their [black] labor," the General concluded, "underlies our wealth."[32]

The type of education that Armstrong prescribed for blacks conformed to his racial prejudices and his views on black labor. As an advocate of the New South philosophy, Samuel Chapman Armstrong held that industry and education were complementary: "Commerce, the law of supply and demand, the necessity of labor, are all educational; railroads, the best of civilizing institutions, are doing a great work for the South."[33] The General thought of blacks primarily in terms of what they could contribute to the economic prosperity of the country. In harmony with the racial economics of his age, Armstrong considered blacks to be inferior, barbaric, and ugly creatures—with a "facial angle," "thicker cranium," "two inch longer arm," and "color of skin" that were all "repulsive," but "no barrier to industry."[34] His belief in the superiority of the Anglo-Saxon to the African race led him to the conclusion that blacks were by nature destined for only one purpose in life. "The Negroes," Armstrong proclaimed, "are to form the working classes. . . ."[35]

The basic idea underlying the educational philosophy of Hampton Institute was the more efficient exploitation of that labor, to fitting the Negro in his place. The General professed that through Hampton, "Southerners could save themselves from a vast vagrancy and secure for themselves a supply of the best labor in the world."[36] The goal of the school, he stated in 1874, "is not to make thorough scholars since the need of the South is for stalwart men and women."[37] He considered this to be quite appropriate for the blacks since, as he put it, "The Negro is naturally expected to do his share in helping to promote the advancement of the Nation at large. . . in the development of the resources of the country."[38]

Northern industry needed more black labor and Hampton helped meet that need. A great void developed in the field of domestic service as many of the Irish, who had comprised the majority of domestic servants in Boston and New York, began to move into the expanding factory system. Others were, perhaps, belatedly listening to Horace Greeley's advice and going West. "At the North," the General surmised, "the housekeeping question becomes more serious every year."[39] In Armstrong's mind blacks were the natural choice for those positions in domestic service abandoned by the Irish. The training that black women received at Hampton in dusting, cooking, and making beds made them perfect for domestic service. And the male students were strong and well fit for the rigors of industrial work.[40] The Founder had the school function as a conduit for Northern employers who wanted blacks. The *Southern Workman* served as "a convenient medium of communication" between Northern employers and Southern black workers. In an article in the *Workman* titled "To Northern Employers and Southern Workers," the institute boasted of its role in supplying to the North "faithful" and "competent" black laborers.[41]

When the number of workers drawn off to the North reached

a point that Samuel Chapman Armstrong thought detrimental to the South, he sought to cut off the spigot. Since the end of Reconstruction the exodus of blacks to the North from every section of the South had gradually increased. By the last decade of the nineteenth century, thousands of blacks were leaving the South yearly. The South was losing too much of its treasured labor force. Armstrong began suggesting that blacks "cast down their bucket" where they were. The General now said that the North had nothing to offer the Negro. He told them that they could not hope to compete with the immigrants, who increased in number each day as more arrived at Castle Garden. In 1891 he lashed out in the *Southern Workman* at the exodus fever, telling blacks that once they "begin to see more clear and straight . . . they will realize that the industrial freedom which he [the black] enjoys at the South is far greater than in the North." Armstrong advised them that the mass migration to the North was senseless because the unions controlled the jobs. He said that in the North, "The white man is at the mercy of the trade unions; the black man in the South is not. . . ."[42]

In his list of advantages to staying put, the Founder neglected to mention the neo-slave system facing blacks in the South. The destruction of the peculiar institution no more freed the slaves than it severed the southland from dependency on black labor. The new slavery consisted of sharecropping, debt peonage, and convict lease supplemented by jim crow and down-home racism. For blacks the old rhyme still held true:

> *Nought's a nought,*
> *figure' a figure;*
> *All for de white man—*
> *None for de nigger.*[43]

Some Southerners advocated additional stringent methods to guarantee the subserviency of blacks. In South Carolina, Mississippi, Georgia, Arkansas, Louisiana, Alabama, and Virginia, whites organized armed brigades to keep the blacks in line. The *New York Times* reported that in several of the cotton states, white leaders "expressed the belief that the Negro, to be made useful, must be kept in a state little better than bondage, in short, as close to a condition of slavery as possible." To bring this result, the *Times* continued, "the Rifle Clubs of South Carolina and a number of the most prominent Democrats in Alabama and Louisiana are engaged in a determined effort to organize the Old Labor Leagues, and secure such legislative enactments as will place the unfortunate black laborers absolutely under their control."[44]

Hampton Institute defended the South's treatment of blacks. The *Southern Workman* defined the Compromise of 1877 as the watershed between slavery and freedom. According to the *Workman*, the Negro's "own ignorance and vices" kept him from progressing.[45] The school reported that blacks suffered most from "intemperance; rum is doing him [the black] more harm than prejudice; immorality is a curse tenfold greater than Rifle Clubs or Labor Leagues. . . . 'Southern hate,' so freely referred to in political papers, is a minor factor in the forces that keep the negro down."[46] Hampton maintained that true Southerners, the good white folks, the "best element" of the South, "pledged" themselves to the black's "protection and education."[47] The Founder said, "The Southern Negro has the best wishes of his white neighbors."[48] He wrote to an associate in the North: "The Southerner is kind to the Negro, likes to be served by him, and would divide with him his last loaf of bread."[49] Armstrong, moreover, invited Northern blacks to come South: "The Negro who wishes to do a man's work goes South to live. There is his empire. He may make, in some cases, more money in the North, but accumulates more in the South, where relatively he is more of a man, from his importance as a voter and labourer."[50]

The General conceded that blacks faced some injustices in the South but added that the same held true for whites. He blamed the trade and credit system. General Armstrong claimed that within that system lay the *real* enemy of both blacks and poor whites. "Jews," he declared, "are the most conspicuous class of traders, whose record in the South resembles, somewhat, their record in other countries. Both white and coloured feel the iron hand of these men."[51]

The school recommended that blacks put their trust in the Anglo-Saxon. Hollis B. Frissell, chaplain under Armstrong and later principal of Hampton Institute, noted: "While the colored man has much more of a certain sort of respect for the white man than the Indian has, his suspicion of the white race is no less."[52] Frissell, like other Hampton proponents, believed that blacks owed a debt of gratitude to the Anglo-Saxon in general and the Southern Anglo-Saxon in particular for the "helpful influences of slavery, which brought to masses of barbarians some knowledge of regular work, of the English language, and of the Christian religion. . . ." But to the school's dismay, it was "nevertheless true that slavery produced in the hearts of the Negro race a belief in the injustice of the ruling race. . . ."[53] Henry W. Grady, editor of the *Atlanta Constitution* and a supporter of Hampton Institute, urged blacks to forgive and forget. In a letter to Booker T. Washington published in the *Southern Workman*, Grady declared, "There need be no hostility either of action or sentiment between the white and colored people in the South. Their interests are identical and they should be friends in the best sense of the word."[54]

But not equals. Samuel Chapman Armstrong himself was a staunch anti-amalgamationist. "The races," he said, "have been on far too intimate terms."[55] The slave's labor was not the only commodity that the slave-master ravished. Black women paid dearly. The mulatto population of the South was a pointed reminder as to just how intimate the races had been. Mulattoes comprised the vast majority of the student body at Hampton. "Less than half of our Negroes are pure blooded," the General reported; "Afro-American is perhaps the best word for them."[56] No matter how they were termed—Afro-American, black, pickaninie, or just plain Negro—their place in Southern society was unquestionably at the bottom. The Founder stressed that blacks stay in their place. And nothing bothered him more than miscegenation, which he termed "deplorable."[57] He called his students' attention to the example of Frederick Douglass, who, he said, "lost caste with his people when he married a white wife."[58] Armstrong's concern was not over what might be in the best interest of blacks. Rather, he believed that whites were

superior and, therefore, that the two races should remain separate. Where the General and Hampton Institute stood is clear
from what he said in 1891: "Social equality is not dreamed
of."[59]

Blacks received an education at Hampton Institute that in
every way conformed to the status quo. There was no danger,
as some whites feared, that industrial schooling would make
the black competitive with the skilled labor force of the South.
One student of Hampton observed that, contrary to popular
belief about General Armstrong's views, he did not expect most
black laborers to become artisans.[60] The General told blacks
that the temporal salvation of the colored race was to be won
out of the ground.[61] They were to be agricultural laborers or
the unskilled menial work force of industry. Samuel Chapman
Armstrong thought it a waste of time to attempt to train blacks
beyond the most basic rudiments. He opposed such academic
institutions as Howard, Fisk, Atlanta, and Wilberforce—schools
that sought to train blacks for professional careers. Having no
faith in the black's intellectual capacity, Armstrong proclaimed

> An English course embracing reading and elocution,
> geography and mathematics, history, the sciences,
> the study of the mother-tongue and its literature,
> the leading principles of mental and moral science,
> and of political economy, would, I think, make a
> curriculum that would exhaust the best powers of
> nineteen-twentieths of those who would for years
> to come enter the Institute.[62]

Through industrial education the General hoped to control
the blacks, not raise them to a level of parity with whites.
Armstrong proceeded with the greatest amount of care. "The
darky," he confided, "is an ugly thing to manage."[63] He was
careful to give his students a limited education, just enough to
fit them to their prescribed station in society and no more.
"Over education" the Founder defined as one of the salient
"dangers with the weak races. . . . For the average [black] pupil," he contended, "too much is as bad as too little."[64]

They could, however, have as much military training as they wanted. Each male student was assigned to a company in the Hampton Institute battalion. The purpose of this instruction, General Armstrong made quite clear, "is not intended to make soldiers out of our students, or create warlike spirit." The General pointed out that the students drilled "without arms."[65] Armstrong's faith in military discipline stemmed from his experience as commander of a black regiment during the Civil War; and he maintained that the black pupil like the black soldier could be "readily transformed under wise control" and the result would be "good conduct generally."[66] Through military instruction, Armstrong intended to teach the student a "respect for law" and "a proper regard for authority."[67] The Hampton administration called it "a splendid thing" that the young men receive military instruction.[68] With its emphasis on regulation, order, system, and obedience, military training played a vital role in fostering those characteristics that Samuel Chapman Armstrong deemed appropriate for blacks.[69]

Even the program of physical education at the institute played an essential role in the Hampton process, according to the Founder. The physical education department sought to develop a spirit of "keen rivalry" among the students.[70] The head of the Department of Physical Education for Girls reported that the purpose of the athletic activities for the students was to build "good sportsmanship, honor and fair play, loyalty, cooperation, and generosity to opponents."[71] The program fit the Founder's wishes. Every activity of the institute, Peabody noted, "the class-room, the trade-school, the farm, and the church are co-ordinated agents of education as it is conceived at Hampton."[72]

While the Founder's favorite statement was "the education of the head, hand, and heart," he considered the latter to be the most important. "There can be no question as to the paramount necessity of teaching the vital precepts of the Christian faith."[73] At Hampton all phases of institutional life revolved around religion.[74] The General often said that the black students needed a regime that controlled them twenty-four hours each day, and he felt religion helped to do just that.[75]

The institute's rigorous emphasis on religion awed both students and visitors alike. "When I registered at Hampton," a woman student recalled, "I thought I was well acquainted with the three R's, but I have found that the three R's of importance are Religion, Respect for Rules, and Responsibility."[76] Dr. Samuel Eliot of the Boston School Committee, upon returning home from a visit to Hampton Institute, remarked: "There is a moral training in that School I hardly dare to claim for any institution in this part of the country."[77]

The Founder's intent was to inculcate the students with those religious qualities appropriate for their place in the South. Students at Hampton were required to attend the religious services held each day in the school church, and every student was assigned a seat so that attendance could be easily monitored.[78] Mostly they heard about the need to be good Christians and about practices that the local white churches failed to live up to when they refused to admit Hampton students.[79] Armstrong never challenged the churches for their failure to practice the brotherly love that they preached, because first, he was a proponent of segregation, and second, he did not want to set an example of assertiveness for his students. Armstrong said that he did not want to take a chance of "encourag[ing] the blacks in their already threatening inclination to self-assertion and racial hostility."[80] He offered this advice to those under his charge: "Real progress is not in increase of wealth or power, but is gained in wisdom, self-control, in guiding principles, and in Christian ideas."[81] J.L.M. Curry, an influential Southerner and a leading advocate of industrial education, summed up the motives behind the emphasis on religion at Hampton better than anyone else: "The Negro could be both Christianized and educated, and that upon his Christianization and his right education rested . . . the safety and prosperity of the white race with whom he dwelt."[82]

The favorite hymns of the Hampton students indicate that the Founder's religious philosophy was accepted.

> *Ain't Goin' Study War No More*
> *1*
> *Goin to lay down my sword an' shield,*
> *Down by de riber side.*

> *Chorus*
> *I ain't goin' to study war no more,*
> *Ain't goin' study war no more.*
> *2*
> *Going to try on my starry crown,*
> *Down by de riber side.*
> *3*
> *Going to try on my long white robe,*
> *Down by de riber side.*[83]

It might be argued that Christianity and all religions advocate pacifism. But the holy scriptures speak also of the triumph of good over evil. Religious scholars have debated the issue of how that triumph is to come about. Hampton students engaged in no such debate. They were taught not to think in terms of triumphs or conquests. The stratagem impressed upon them for attacking the evils and wrongs of society was to turn the other cheek and seek comfort in Jesus.

> *I Am Troubled in Mind*
>
> *I am troubled,*
> *I am troubled in mind.*
> *If Jesus don't help me*
> *I surely will die.*
> *1*
> *O Jesus, my Savior,*
> *On thee I depend;*
> *When troubles are near me*
> *You will be my true friend.*
> *2*
> *And when I am in trouble*
> *And laden with grief,*
> *To Jesus, my Savior*
> *I will go for relief.*[84]

Whether out of a need to escape the evils of the South or out of true belief, Hampton students looked forward to the hereafter.

In Bright Mansions Above

In bright mansions above,
In bright mansions above,
Lord, I wan't t' live up yonder,
In bright mansions above.
                1
My mother's gone to glory
I wan't t' go there too, Lord,
I wan't' live up yonder,
In bright mansions above.
                2
My sister's gone to glory,
I wan't t' go there too, Lord,
I wan't t' live up yonder,
In bright mansions above.
                3
My Saviour's gone to glory,
I wan't t' go there too, Lord,
I wan't' live up yonder
In bright mansions above. [85]

It does seem certain that institutionalized Christianity, with
its emphasis on a supreme being who is portrayed as white and
who has made "man" in his own image, could hardly give its
"other worshippers," especially blacks, reinforcements for
healthy psychological development. It is impossible to assess
in exact terms how much of the negativism of Christianity
Hampton students internalized.

Lord, I Want to Be a Christian
                1
Lord, I want to be a Christian,
In-a my heart, in-a my heart,
Lord, I want to be a Christian,
In-a my heart.
    . . . .
Lord, I want to be like Jesus,

> *Lord, I want to be like Jesus,*
> *In-a my heart, in-a my heart,*
> *In-a my heart.*[86]

Strict religious instruction, psalm singing, and constant prayer did have some discernable results. It was reported that after leaving Hampton the students went forth to make peace between the races.[87] They were quite successful, no doubt, because as one report stated, "Nearly every graduate conducts a Sunday school and many of them are useful as evangelists. . . . They seldom seek [political] office, but devoted themselves to the real welfare of their people."[88] From every state in the nation Hampton graduates wrote to the Founder, informing him that they were spreading the Hampton idea, working hard at whatever task was given, and leading a Christian life.[89]

Christians in the Hampton area supported Armstrong's ideas. Local white Christians showed their appreciation of the work being done at the school by helping to raise the money that enabled the institute to establish the first black-student YMCA in the United States[90] on its campus. Black Christians supported the Founder's work and aided him in disseminating the Hampton ideology throughout the black community. The *Southern Workman* reported that the colored pastors themselves thus became important allies and helpers in the work of Hampton Institute.[91]

The Hampton graduates, however, remained the school's primary asset. They were living, breathing testimonials of what Hampton could do, and proud of it. Many of Armstrong's former students wrote to him praising his foresight. One graduate said he believed that blacks who felt themselves better than the menial labor Hampton advocated were "shiftless, and ought to be despised."[92] Two graduates declared in a joint letter that the Founder's philosophy of industrial schooling for blacks was twenty-five years ahead of its time. "Your example, your picture, your personal and business letters to [us]," they wrote, "are lasting spurs to urge one on in obedience to your command. . . ."[93] The *Southern Workman* carried letters from blacks all over the country praising the work of Hampton Institute

and its graduates.[94] Armstrong told the truth when he said,
"The black race is strikingly responsive to the influence" of the
Hampton graduates.[95]

Ninety percent of the graduates became teachers, which made
Hampton's influence on the black race profound. As teachers,
they carried the Hampton idea to every sinew of the black South.
It was reported that during the school year ending in 1880,
Hampton graduates had taught between 15,000 and 20,000
students.[96] They were allowed to teach because the colored
teacher could be counted on to work in harmony with the prevailing Southern order of things. It seemed likely if not inevi-
table to many Southern whites that blacks were going to be educated. The real concern, then, was that they receive the right
type of education, the kind that would keep them in their
place. The Hampton-trained black pedagogue, armed with the
industrial education philosophy, promised to do just that.
"There is a great and growing demand for colored teachers
and colored schools," Armstrong said; "they are not obnoxious
to southern men. . . ."[97]

Southern whites feared the Northern schoolmarm. "Southern men will not, as a rule, teach Negroes," the General noted,
"and there are insuperable obstacles and strong objections to
a general supply of northern teachers."[98] White Southerners
believed that Northern teachers would have a bad influence
on the blacks, that they might attempt to educate them beyond their station in life. "A Northern school-teacher might
impart refinement and consecration," Francis Peabody declared, "but she might also encourage the delusion that book-
learning was better than manual industry, and that freedom
from slavery meant freedom from work."[99] J.L.M. Curry said,
"The average New England teacher approached the task, however sincerely, as if the Negro were simply a backward white
man, an untaught Mayflower descendant."[100] Armstrong
agreed. His racial thinking was in harmony with that of the
white South. He was critical of missionary teachers who did
not abide by the Southern color line. "The South will accept
and tolerate colored teachers—never the New England girls (in
some cases I don't wonder at it)," he said. "The Yankee

schoolmarms, by their fervent preaching of equalitarian doctrines, alienated large and important elements in Southern society. . . ."[101]

The Southerner's fear was not entirely justified, however. It was true that "Negro uplift" were bywords of many of the Northern teachers who came South. The missionary teacher George Hyde was openly critical of those who advocated that "modified slavery" was best for blacks. He promised to do all he could to make the freedmen unsuitable for reenslavement.[102] However, Miss Jane S. Woolsey, for example, who came from New York to teach in the South, had a reputation of being conservative in her thinking on racial matters. She sided with the Armstrong school of thought, settled at Hampton Institute, and there established the Girl's Industrial Department.[103] Many of the Northern teachers who came South had some of the same predilections about blacks that Southern whites did. Their racial bigotry, however, was couched in humanitarianism, in a philosophy of black inferiority that George M. Frederickson has described as "romantic racialism."[104] Moreover, while industrial education was not professed by most missionary teachers, it was the American Missionary Association itself that had been instrumental in establishing Hampton Institute and had aided the school in its climb to prominence by giving it financial support.

The South's "Northernophobia," nevertheless, persisted, especially in the area of politics. Southerners held a general fear that the Northern teachers, all of whom were Republicans, would work to free the black's political strength and rally it against the Democratic South.[105] The *Virginia Patron* carried a scathing editorial on the Northern influence at Hampton Institute. The editor believed that the school taught blacks "to hate the native whites," and to assert themselves politically.[106] strong emphatically denied the charges. He said that, on the contrary, the aim of Hampton Institute was "to build up and create conservative tendencies . . . among the negroes many of whom have foolish and unjust notions about the whites."[107]

The Founder opposed black political activism. The year 1876 marked the end of Reconstruction and the beginning of a sec-

ond nadir in black political participation in the South.[108] Where
Armstrong stood is clear from his support of the Great Compromise and the conciliatory presidency of Rutherford B. Hayes.[109]
The Founder contended that the Republican party was "smitten
with disease" and that "the Democratic party has the most intelligence in the South."[110] He agreed with those who advocated
that the South was best left to Southern wisdom and the vote
best left in the hands of white men. "Political power being
placed in his [the black's] hand," the General said, "he becomes
the prey of the demagogue or attempts that low part himself.
In either case he is the victim of his greatest weakness—vanity."[111]
Armstrong pointed to what he considered to be the record of
black politicians during Reconstruction, or what he termed the
corrupt, extravagant, high-handed politics of the eight years
after the war. He added, "The general demoralization during
the rule of the blacks was unspeakably bad; civilization could
hardly stand up before it."[112] He advised blacks not to assert
themselves politically. "Negro doctors, lawyers and ministers
are steadily and widely establishing themselves, while Negro
political leaders are going to the bad, in the Southern States:
of the first, a better negro class is forming: of the last a class
sedimentary and worthless."[113] According to Armstrong, politics did not touch the "bread and meat question" of blacks
"except as, through bad government, lawlessness and unpun-
ished homicide keep away enterprise and capital. . . . The mineral, lumber and planting industries of the South find in them
[blacks] . . . 'the best labor in the world.' "[114] In 1891 he
wrote, "Clear headed non-political colored men do not wish,
just now, whatever supremacy their vote would entitle them
to have."[115] He called it "most unfortunate" that some blacks
followed the advice of political activists. The case of the "blind
leading the blind," as the General put it, "is already seen in
the belief" among blacks "that political rights are better obtained by political warfare. . . . How to withstand these dangers
. . . is one of the problems most urgently pressing on Southern
society."[116]

Industrial education was the answer. "Only the most vigorous
and wise educational effort," Armstrong proclaimed, "only an
active interest in mental and moral welfare on the part of good

men of all sections, will save Virginia and other States from being pushed by nearly a million well-meaning, but blind and incapable Negro voters. . . ."[117] He told his black students to restrain themselves from the lure of political activity. "Patience is better than politics, and industry a shorter road to civil rights," Armstrong advised in the *Southern Workman.*[118]

The issue was not that the black be allowed to vote but that he be qualified to vote.[119] This was the political philosophy professed at Hampton Institute, and the Founder believed that it should be adopted throughout the black South. He wrote a friend in the North, telling him of his success at Hampton in shaping the thinking of his students along this line: " 'Give us not more rights but more light' said a Hampton graduate the other day."[120] He offered other testimonials to Hampton's accomplishments. "The whites say the negroes don't steal nearly as much as formerly," he wrote, "that they work better than ever and don't say much about hard times."[121]

The Founder's most impressive example of the institute's success in directing its students' political thinking centered on the issue of the so-called "Force Bill," introduced by Representative Henry Cabot Lodge in 1890. The bill would have sent federal officers to register black voters, thus overcoming the exclusionary tactics of the South. In short, it proposed to make the southland abide by the Fifteenth Amendment. The bill, however, was denounced and killed in the Senate. The General queried Hampton's student body on the "Force Bill." The next day he reported: "And for all that the majority of my negro students voted and wisely, the other day against the so-called 'Force Bill'. Ideas are doing their work."[122] In light of what was taking place at Hampton Institute, Armstrong stated the gospel when he remarked, "The South educated the black man as a measure of self-protection."[123]

The Founder was in harmony with the South's traditions. Exemplifying one of the most sacred Southern prejudices, a dislike of statism, Armstrong opposed federal aid to education. He won great popularity in Virginia when he joined forces with Edward P. Chase of the *Evening Post* and fought against the National Aid to Education Bill sponsored by Senator Blair of New Hampshire in 1888.[124] The General believed that the South-

erners could and would take care of their own problems and
in the best way for them. The government, in his estimation,
did a fine job in building custom houses, railroads, and bridges,
but on too many issues it was "critical and obstructive, rather
than helpful."[125]

Southerners applauded what Samuel Chapman Armstrong
and Hampton Institute stood for. In praising the effectiveness
of the school, Atticus Haygood, President of Emory College,
said, "I state again that the Negro is becoming more and more
an intelligent laborer, more and more a good citizen. . . ."[126]
James MacAlister, a friend of the South, thought that Hampton
demonstrated what he had "always believed to be the solution"
to the Negro problem.[127] The state of Virginia's financial assistance to the institute increased on a regular basis.[128] The Virginia
Legislature offered its thanks for the school's work with blacks.[129]

Vulgar racists could rally behind Hampton and its Founder.
Former slave-masters advocated that schools similar to Hampton Institute be established throughout the black South.[130]
The institute's list of friends included some of the harshest
white supremacists in the South. Governor Seay of Alabama
believed in the Hampton idea.[131] D. H. Chamberlain, Governor
of South Carolina, who was an outspoken race supremacist,
wrote, "I believe, and I have often said, that Gen. Armstrong
and Hampton Institute have done and are doing more to solve
successfully the problem of the relations of the negro to our
society and Government than any other single agency." He suggested that everyone "give his utmost aid to Gen. Armstrong's
work."[132]

There were blacks who understood and opposed what Hampton stood for. Scholars mention the names of W.E.B. Du Bois
and William Monroe Trotter as opponents of industrial schooling. The black community of Hampton, Virginia, had its own
local challenger to the industrial education idea. William Roscoe
Davis, who was born a slave in Norfolk, Virginia, had come to
the Hampton area during the Civil War. He spoke against the
goals of Hampton Institute. It was clear to him that Armstrong
was offering blacks a "peculiar" education.[133] "If Negroes don't
get any better education than Armstrong is giving them," Davis
warned, "they may as well have stayed in slavery."[134]

Poor whites had mixed feelings about the institute. Many of them supported the school while others opposed it on the general principle that blacks should never be educated. Others remained adamant in their fear that blacks might receive training that would put them above whites in the labor market or at least cause the Negro to think of himself as an equal. Back-country whites in the Hampton area swayed little over the years from their position of hostility toward the school.[135]

Lower-class whites' disapproval of the institute failed to dissuade those who saw in Hampton the proper solution to the "Negro problem." The school's ever-increasing list of supporters included such influential names as: Rutherford B. Hayes, James Garfield, Benjamin Harrison, William Howard Taft, John Wanamaker, Morris K. Jesup, J.L.M. Curry, John F. Slater, Robert Curtis Ogden, and Collis P. Huntington. That Northern big-business men supported the industrial education idea is a point that must be examined in detail elsewhere.

To be sure, Hampton Institute and the schools born of it had a commercial value to Southern industry and Northerners with economic interests in the South. Although it is clear that Samuel Chapman Armstrong did not found the institute for his private economic gain, he did enjoy a comfortable financial existence via the school. Under the name of Hampton Institute, Armstrong had personal holdings in the Hampton Educational Association, the Norfolk & Bramleton Railroad Company, the Colorado Grand Canyon Cattle Company, the Calumet Mining Company, the Bank of Commerce of Norfolk, local tenant farms, and a host of other smaller concerns in Hampton, Virginia, including the area's oyster industry.[136]

William Howard Taft caught the essence of the Hampton idea when he said, "Upon the southern white man depends the solution of the race problem" and "the method of solving it at Hampton" demonstrated to Northerners and Southerners "how possible it is to make his black fellow citizens of the fair South a source of profit, of peace, of law and order, and of general community happiness."[137]

Samuel Chapman Armstrong died in 1893, but his model of schooling for blacks survived. The new champion of the industrial education idea was a black man. In 1881 this young man,

Armstrong's star pupil, had been given the task of building a school on the Hampton model in Macon County, Alabama. This institute was the "first child" of Hampton, and the school's young principal "was to General Armstrong as was Timothy to Paul."[138] The school was Tuskegee Institute and the man, Booker Taliaferro Washington.

NOTES

1. *Annual Report of the Principal and Officers of Hampton Normal and Agricultural Institute, 1872* (Hampton, Va.: Hampton Institute Press, 1872); Isaac Fisher, "The Unique Educational Philosophy of Samuel Chapman Armstrong," Unpublished Manuscript, *Armstrong Family Papers*, Williams College, 1933, p. 167.

2. *Annual Report of the Principal and Officers of Hampton Normal and Agricultural Institute, 1881* (Hampton, Va.: Hampton Institute Press, 1881); *Southern Workman*, June 1881, p. 63.

3. Francis Greenwood Peabody, *Education For Life: The Story of Hampton Institute* (New York: Doubleday, Page and Company, 1918), pp. 274-275.

4. See August Meier, *Negro Thought in America, 1880-1915* (Ann Arbor, Mich.: The University of Michigan Press, 1963), pp. 85-88.

5. Richard Armstrong to Reuben Chapman, 8 September 1848, *Armstrong Family Papers*, Williams College.

6. Suzanne Carson, "Samuel Chapman Armstrong: Missionary to the South" (Ph.D. Dissertation, Johns Hopkins University, 1952), p. 20.

7. Mrs. Clarissa Chapman Armstrong to Reuben Chapman, 1 April 1836, *Armstrong Family Papers*.

8. Richard Armstrong to Reuben Chapman, 11 October 1847, *Armstrong Family Papers*.

9. Ibid., 21 July 1843.

10. *Ludlow Collection*, Helen Ludlow, ed., *Personal Memoirs and Letters of General Samuel Chapman Armstrong: Hawaii, Williams, War, Hampton*, Vol. IV, 1894, p. 860.

11. Samuel Chapman Armstrong to Mrs. Clarissa Chapman Armstrong, 13 November 1860, *Armstrong Family Papers*.

12. *Ludlow Collection* 3, p. 772.

13. *Southern Workman*, June 1892, p. 79.

14. *Ludlow Collection* 3, p. 619.

15. *American Missionary Magazine* 13 (June 1896), p. 123.

16. Samuel Chapman Armstrong to Howard Potter, 3 February 1891, p. 4, *Armstrong Family Papers*.

17. *Ludlow Collection* 3, p. 646.

18. Fisher, p. 132.

19. *Southern Workman*, 15 August 1891, p. 5.

20. Peabody, p. 244.

21. Pamphlet titled, *Everyday Life at Hampton Institute* (Hampton, Va.: Hampton Institute Press, n.d.), p. 6. *Samuel Chapman Armstrong Collection*, Hampton Institute.

22. *Southern Workman*, February 1880, p. 1; Samuel Chapman Armstrong, *Education for Life* (Hampton, Va.: Hampton Institute Press, n.d.), pp. 37-38. *Samuel Chapman Armstrong Collection*.

23. Carrie Alberta Lyford, "Hampton Institute," *Report of the Department of the Interior, Bureau of Education*, Bulletin no. 23 (Washington, D.C.: Government Printing Office, 1923), p. 78.

24. *Southern Workman*, June 1879, p. 63, and September 1880, p. 3; Samuel Chapman Armstrong, *Education for Life*, p. 38.

25. *Southern Workman*, July 1873, p. 4.

26. Ibid., May 1874, pp. 21-22.

27. Ibid., July 1873, p. 4.

28. Ibid., March 1874, p. 2.

29. *Ludlow Collection* 3, p. 772.

30. Samuel Chapman Armstrong to Howard Potter, 3 February 1891, p. 1, *Armstrong Family Papers*.

31. *Southern Workman*, July 1883, p. 76, and passim.

32. *Ludlow Collection* 3, p. 772; 4, p. 855.

33. *Southern Workman*, June 1884, p. 65.

34. Samuel Chapman Armstrong to Howard Potter, 3 February 1891, p. 6, *Armstrong Family Papers*.

35. Samuel Chapman Armstrong, *Ideas on Education* (Hampton, Va.: Hampton Institute Press, 1908), p. 4. Issued for the Armstrong League of Hampton Workers.

36. Fisher, p. 97.

37. *Rochester Democrat*, 30 March 1874. Clipping in the *Armstrong Family Papers*.

38. *Annual Report of the Principal and Officers of Hampton Normal and Agricultural Institute, 1881*, p. 11.

39. *Southern Workman*, December 1872, p. 2.

40. Ibid.; *Ludlow Collection* 3, p. 547. Sarah J. Walter, "The Whittier Training School," *Report of the Department of the Interior, Bureau of Education*, Bulletin no. 23 (Washington, D.C.: Government Printing Office, 1923), p. 38.

41. *Southern Workman*, December 1872, p. 2.

42. Ibid., 6 June 1891, p. 215.

43. Ibid., February 1878, pp. 10-11; Richard Wright, *12 Million Black*

Voices: A Folk History of the Negro in the United States (New York: Viking Press, 1941), p. 42.

44. As cited in *Southern Workman,* February 1878, pp. 10-11.

45. Ibid.

46. Ibid.

47. Ibid.

48. Samuel Chapman Armstrong to Howard Potter, 3 February 1891, p. 6, *Armstrong Family Papers.*

49. Ibid., p. 1.

50. *Annual Report of the Principal and Officers of Hampton Normal and Agricultural Institute, 1881,* p. 5.

51. Samuel Chapman Armstrong to Howard Potter, 3 February 1891, p. 5, *Armstrong Family Papers.*

52. Hollis B. Frissell, "Our Responsibility to Undeveloped Races," *Report of the American Missionary Association,* Bulletin no. 23 (Hampton, Va.: Hampton Institute Press, n.d.), p. 5. Copy in the *Armstrong Family Papers.*

53. Ibid.

54. *Southern Workman,* February 1887, p. 22.

55. Samuel Chapman Armstrong to Howard Potter, 3 February 1891, p. 1, *Armstrong Family Papers.*

56. Ibid.

57. Ibid., p. 4.

58. Ibid., p. 6.

59. Ibid.

60. Peabody, pp. xiv-xv.

61. *Catalogue of the Hampton Normal and Agricultural Institute, 1871-72* (Hampton, Va.: Hampton Institute Press, 1872), p. 22; *Southern Workman,* July 1883, p. 195; *Annual Report of the Principal and Officers of Hampton Normal and Agricultural Institute, 1883,* p. 11; *Proceedings of the National Education Association, 1872,* p. 176.

62. *Ludlow Collection* 3, p. 673.

63. Samuel Chapman Armstrong to Emma Armstrong, 8 January 1878, *Armstrong Family Papers.*

64. "Address by Samuel Chapman Armstrong Before the National Education Association, 1872," *Armstrong Family Papers;* Samuel Chapman Armstrong, *Education For Life,* p. 20.

65. Cited in Peabody, p. 135.

66. Samuel Chapman Armstrong, *Ideas on Education,* p. 6.

67. Major Allen W. Washington, Commandant, Hampton Institute, "Discipline," *Report of the Department of the Interior, Bureau of Education,* Bulletin no. 23 (Washington, D.C.: Government Printing Office, 1923), p. 101.

68. Ibid., p. 99.

69. Peabody, p. 135.

70. Charles H. Williams, "Hampton Institute," *Report of the Department of the Interior, Bureau of Education,* Bulletin no. 23 (Washington, D.C.: Government Printing Office, 1923), p. 93.

71. Olive B. Rowell, ibid., p. 97.

72. Peabody, p. xvi.

73. Samuel Chapman Armstrong, *Religious Training* (Hampton, Va.: Hampton Institute Press, n.d.), p. 12. Copies in *Armstrong Collection* and *Armstrong Family Papers.*

74. Washington, "Discipline," p. 99.

75. Samuel Chapman Armstrong, *Ideas on Education,* p. 6; "Education of the Character" in *Education For Life,* p. 40; *Southern Workman,* February 1882, p. 5.

76. Cited in Peabody, p. 258.

77. *Ludlow Collection* 5, p. 1150.

78. Washington, "Discipline," p. 99.

79. Herbert Welsch, "Samuel Chapman Armstrong," *Educational Review* (1893), p. 118; Jane Stuart Woolsey to Samuel Chapman Armstrong, December 1869, *Armstrong Collection.*

80. Peabody, pp. 284-285.

81. Samuel Chapman Armstrong, *Education For Life,* p. 38.

82. Cited in Peabody, p. 53.

83. *Some Songs of the Hampton Institute Quartette* (Hampton, Va.: Hampton Institute Press, n.d.), p. 17. Copies in *Armstrong Collection* and *Armstrong Family Papers.*

84. Ibid.

85. Ibid., p. 20.

86. Ibid., p. 38.

87. T. C. Walker, "Development in the Tidewater Counties of Virginia," *The Annals of the American Academy* (n.d.), p. 30. Copy in *Armstrong Family Papers.*

88. Walter Aery, "Hampton Institute," *Report of the Department of the Interior, Bureau of Education,* Bulletin no. 23 (Washington, D.C.: Government Printing Office, 1923), pp. 113-114.

89. *Southern Workman:* May 1876, p. 38; July 1876, p. 54; August 1876, p. 63; September 1876, p. 71; November 1876, p. 87; February 1877, p. 14; March 1877, p. 20; April 1877, p. 30; May 1877, p. 38; June 1877, p. 46; August 1877, p. 59; September 1877, p. 67; January 1878, p. 5; May 1878, p. 38; July 1878, p. 52; August 1878, p. 60; September 1878, p. 68; October 1878, p. 76; November 1878, p. 84; December 1878, p. 92; January 1879, p. 6; February 1879, p. 18; March 1879, p. 30; April 1879, p. 42; May 1879, p. 54; June 1879, p. 68; July

1879, p. 76; October 1879, p. 100; December 1879, p. 122; January 1881, p. 6; February 1881, p. 18; March 1881, p. 30; April 1881, p. 42; June 1881, p. 66; November 1881, p. 110; December 1881, p. 122; March 1882, p. 80; April 1882, p. 42; May 1882, p. 54; July 1882, p. 78; August 1882, p. 86; September 1882, p. 94; October 1882, p. 102; November 1882, p. 110; December 1882, p. 123; January 1883, p. 6; February 1883, p. 18; March 1883, p. 30; April 1883, p. 42; May 1883, p. 54; July 1883, p. 80; August 1883, p. 88; September 1883, p. 96; October 1883, p. 104; November 1883, p. 112; December 1883, p. 124; January 1884, p. 6; February 1884, p. 18; March 1884, p. 31; April 1884, p. 42; May 1884, p. 54; July 1884, p. 82; August 1884, p. 90; September 1884, p. 98; October 1884, p. 106; November 1884, p. 114; December 1884, p. 126; January 1885, p. 6; February 1885, p. 18; March 1885, p. 30; April 1885, p. 42; May 1885, p. 54; July 1885, p. 80; September 1885, p. 96; October 1885, p. 104; November 1885, p. 114; December 1885, p. 126; January 1886, p. 6; February 1886, p. 18; March 1886, p. 30; April 1886, p. 42; May 1886, p. 53; July 1886, p. 80; September 1886, p. 96; October 1886, p. 104; November 1886, p. 114; January 1887, p. 6; February 1887, p. 18; March 1887, p. 30; May 1887, p. 54; July 1887, p. 78; August 1887, p. 85; September 1887, p. 93; October 1887, p. 101; November 1887, p. 112; December 1887, p. 124; January 1888, p. 5; February 1888, p. 17; March 1888, p. 29; April 1888, p. 41; May 1888, p. 53; July 1888, p. 78; August 1888, p. 35; October 1888, p. 101; December 1888, p. 124; January 1889, p. 6; February 1889, p. 17; March 1889, p. 30; April 1889, pp. 45-46; November 1889, p. 114; December 1889, p. 126; January 1890, p. 6; February 1890, p. 17; March 1890, p. 29; 1 April 1890, p. 41; 1 May 1890, p. 53; 1 August 1890, p. 87; September 1890, p. 94; November 1890, p. 113; December 1890, p. 125; February 1891, p. 149; March 1891, p. 161; April 1891, p. 173; May 1891, p. 185; August 1891, p. 219; November 1891, p. 245; December 1891, p. 257; January 1892, p. 7; October 1892, p. 153; December 1892, p. 183; February 1893, p. 29; March 1893, p. 43; May 1893, p. 75.

90. Warren K. Blodgett, "The Agricultural School," *Report of the Department of the Interior, Bureau of Education,* Bulletin no. 23 (Washington, D.C.: Government Printing Office, 1923), p. 58.

91. *Southern Workman,* June 1886, p. 73.

92. Ibid., August 1872, p. 2.

93. George W. and Clara T. Brandom to Samuel Chapman Armstrong, 31 January 1892, *Armstrong Family Papers.*

94. See n. 92.

95. *Ludlow Collection* 4, pp. 907-908.

96. *Annual Report of the Principal and Officers of Hampton Normal and Agricultural Institute, 1880,* p. 8; Alrutheus Ambush Taylor, *The*

Negro in the Reconstruction of Virginia (New York: Russell and Russell, [1926] 1969), p. 170.

97. *Proceedings of the National Education Association, 1872,* p. 175.

98. Ibid.

99. Peabody, p. 291.

100. Cited in Peabody, p. 291.

101. Samuel Chapman Armstrong to Mary Jane Armstrong, 22 November 1866, *Armstrong Family Papers; Ludlow Collection* 3, p. 569.

102. George Hyde to Whiting, 21 February 1862, *American Missionary Association Collection,* Fisk University.

103. *Ludlow Collection* 3, p. 643.

104. George M. Fredrickson, *The Black Image in the White Mind: The Debate on Afro-American Character and Destiny, 1817-1914* (New York: Harper and Row, 1971), pp. 99-129.

105. Peabody, p. 291.

106. Samuel Chapman Armstrong to Editor, *Virginia Patron,* 4 May 1876. Copy in *Armstrong Collection.*

107. Ibid.

108. For a discussion, see Rayford W. Logan, *The Betrayal of the Negro* (London: Collier Books, 1969; originally published in 1965 as *The Negro in American Life and Thought: The Nadir, 1877-1901).*

109. *Southern Workman,* May 1874, p. 34.

110. Ibid.

111. *Annual Report of the Principal and Officers of Hampton Normal and Agricultural Institute, 1870,* pp. 44-45; *Ludlow Collection,* Vol. 3, pp. 668-669.

112. *Ludlow Collection* 5, p. 1034.

113. Samuel Chapman Armstrong to Howard Potter, 3 February 1891, p. 2, *Armstrong Family Papers.*

114. Ibid., p. 5.

115. Ibid., p. 8.

116. *Catalogue of the Hampton Normal and Agricultural Institute, 1871-72* (Hampton, Va.: Hampton Institute Press, 1872), p. 21.

117. *Ludlow Collection* 3, p. 773.

118. *Southern Workman,* May 1874, p. 3.

119. *Ludlow Collection* 3, p. 661.

120. Samuel Chapman Armstrong to Howard Potter, 3 February 1891, p. 8, *Armstrong Family Papers.*

121. *Ludlow Collection* 3, p. 661.

122. Samuel Chapman Armstrong to Howard Potter, 3 February 1891, p. 7, *Armstrong Family Papers.*

123. *Southern Workman,* January 1881, p. 5.

124. Edward P. Clark to Samuel Chapman Armstrong, 10 January 1889,

16 January 1889, 16 May 1889, and telegrams, Clark to Armstrong, *Armstrong Family Papers;* Peabody, p. 204.

125. *Annual Report of the Principal and Officers of Hampton Normal and Agricultural Institute, 1883,* p. 7.

126. *Southern Workman,* June 1887, p. 62.

127. Ibid., August 1892, p. 123.

128. Samuel Chapman Armstrong to the Chairman, Committee on Schools and Colleges, of the Virginia Legislature, 2 January 1872, *Armstrong Collection.*

129. *Southern Workman,* May 1887, p. 49.

130. *Ludlow Collection* 4, p. 914.

131. Samuel Chapman Armstrong to Howard Potter, 3 February 1891, p. 8, *Armstrong Family Papers.*

132. *Concerning Hampton Institute* (Hampton, Va.: Hampton Institute Press, n.d.), p. 4. Copy in *Armstrong Collection* and *Armstrong Family Papers.*

133. Arthur P. Davis, "William Roscoe Davis and His Descendants," *Negro History Bulletin* 13 (January 1950), p. 82.

134. Ibid., p. 81.

135. Samuel Chapman Armstrong to Mrs. Clarissa Chapman Armstrong, 30 April 1867, *Armstrong Family Papers;* Mary F. Armstrong and Helen Ludlow, *Hampton and Its Students, By Two of Its Teachers* (New York: Doubleday, 1875), p. 585.

136. Miscellaneous Financial and Business Papers of Samuel Chapman Armstrong, *Armstrong Family Papers.*

137. William Howard Taft, Chief Justice of the United States, and President of Hampton Institute Board of Trustees, "The Influence of Hampton," *Report of the Department of the Interior, Bureau of Education,* Bulletin no. 23 (Washington, D.C.: Government Printing Office, 1923), pp. 3-4.

138. *Ludlow Collection* 4, p. 942.

3

SHINE, BOOKER, SHINE:
THE BLACK OVERSEER
OF TUSKEGEE

Perhaps Paulo Freire had Booker T. Washington in mind when he wrote in his classic study on education, "The oppressed have been destroyed precisely because their situation has reduced them to things. In order to regain their humanity they must cease to be things and fight as men. . . . They cannot enter the struggle as objects in order later to become men."[1] To Booker T. Washington the sensible thing for blacks to do was to fashion a coalition with whites in power to make themselves indispensable "objects" to the prosperity of the nation. His conception of the proper course for blacks rested upon the blacks' own exploitability. He believed that the profit motive dictated American thought and action. Those who proved themselves antagonistic would remain powerless or be annihilated; those who proved themselves of value would be rewarded.[2] Thus, he contended that social, political, and civil rights were secondary issues for blacks—subordinate to and dependent upon the race's economic importance. This philosophy of uplift through submission drew heated criticism from many black leaders. What is not a familiar story is that in his championing of these ideas, Washington alienated many of his Tuskegee students and faculty members and never gained the full support of the white South.

Washington's principalship of Tuskegee Institute, from 1881 to his death in 1915, was during a period dominated by elaborate race theories that justified Anglo-Saxon rule. This was the second coming of pseudoscientific racism, and the mixture of anthropology and Social Darwinism gave even the most well-meaning whites serious doubt about Negro capability. Rayford Logan has aptly labeled this period the Great Nadir.[3]

The effort during this time at "proving" racial superiority (and, therefore, racial inferiority) is exemplified by Thomas Dixon's vicious attack upon the black race in *The Leopard's Spots* (1905). Dixon's book lent support to a view shared by many whites of the North and South that the inferior status of the blacks in America was a direct result of "Negro inferiority." Therefore, it was good sense to keep power out of the hands of an immature and childlike people. Social, economic, and political equality could not be practiced because blacks, by the will of God and nature, were not the equals of whites.

Black intellectuals readily attacked these notions. Archibald H. Grimke, a black man and nephew of the famed Grimke sisters, denounced the pseudoscience as a vile fraud aimed at justifying disfranchisement. Kelly Miller, the renowned Howard University professor and noted black author, challenged Dixon's work on its racism.[4] Aiming directly at the Southern advocacy of the Dixon thesis, Miller said that he wanted to let them know that "the Negro ought not be expected to accept that interpretation of 'social equality' which would rob him of political and civil rights, as well as of educational and industrial opportunity."[5]

Booker T. Washington said that he did not accept the idea of white superiority. On the contrary, he said that at the highest level—that of character and humanity—blacks exceeded whites. "I believe," Washington remarked, "we [blacks] can feel more in five minutes than a white man can in a day."[6] But at the same time, he conceded that whites held the superior position in society.

It seemed to him that capitalist materialism and the profit motive held a higher priority among Americans than humanity and love for their fellow men. The way, then, for blacks to survive would be through nonantagonistic means, to use whatever they possessed "that the white man wants or respects." And what that usually was, Booker T. Washington declared, "is ei-

ther money, or social position, or political influence. . . ."[7]
But since blacks lacked money, social position, and political
influence, they would have to bargain with the one commodity
they held a monopoly on: cheap labor.

> The Negro constitutes in this country one of the most
> compact, reliable, and peaceful elements of labor,
> one which is almost the sole dependence for produc-
> tion in certain directions; and I believe that, if for
> no higher reason than the economic one, the people
> will see that it is worth while to keep so large an ele-
> ment of labor happy, contented and prosperous, by
> surrounding and guarding it with every protection
> and encouragement of the laws.[8]

Washington contended that rights came with economic power.
In black labor he saw the race's bargaining force. If he properly
utilized his strength, Booker Washington predicted, "the Negro
can control labor in the South."[9] However, not by threat, strike,
or unionism would the blacks be given rights, but by being the
nation's most dependable and profitable supply of workers:

> In a word, it seems to me that the whole future of
> our race hinges largely upon the question as to
> whether or not we can make ourselves of such in-
> dispensable service in the community where we
> live that the community will feel they cannot dis-
> pense with our service. If we can succeed in making
> ourselves indispensable, we will find that this fact
> alone will settle a large number of vexing and per-
> plexing questions.[10]

He beseeched blacks to proceed on the white man's terms, follow his advice, and achieve black power. After securing a mone-
tary stake, the next step would be to secure property and thus
become a capitalist.

> Let us go with this kind of development till a negro
> gets to the point, as is already true in some cases,

> where he can get a mortgage on a white man's house
> that he can foreclose at will, well that white man
> will be rather careful about driving that negro away
> from the polls when he attempts to vote, and will
> hesitate about attempting to drive him from a first
> class car.[11]

But Booker T. Washington thought of his people primarily
in terms of their value to whites. He took every opportunity
to remind whites that they depended on blacks:

> It is sometimes said that the destiny of the Negro is
> in the hands of the white people of the South. I say
> that the destiny of the white people of the South is,
> to a large degree, in the hands of the Negro cook!
> The majority of our prosperous Southern white peo-
> ple have their food prepared and served three times
> a day by a Negro woman or girl.[12]

Booker Washington attempted to placate both Anglo-Saxon
and African-American. He said that mutual understanding was
the first step to mutual progress. In his speeches before white
audiences he emphasized "oneness" as loyalty, dependability,
and adaptability. He professed the acquiescence of blacks to
the leadership of whites. Washington told a white Southern
audience:

> For example, in the matter of religion the Negro
> does not cling to his old form of religion as some
> other peoples do who come into America; he at
> once lays aside his old beliefs and adapts himself
> to the religions of the people in his own commu-
> nity. If the other people there are Baptists he be-
> comes a Baptist too; if they are Methodists he
> becomes a Methodist; if they are Presbyterians, he
> becomes a Presbyterian; and if they are Episcopal-
> ians—why, he even becomes an Episcopalian! In the
> matter of language he does not cling to his tribal

> dialect, he does not cling to his African tongue as
> the Italian and German and Russian Jew do to their
> languages. He speaks English—or makes a brave at-
> tempt to speak it. The same is true of other things.[13]

In attempting to sell blacks on the idea that the Southern states were not the best place for them. Washington empha- sized what he considered to be the most important advantages to life in the South for blacks. In the South, he said, blacks can work the land, and "the soil will yield her riches as quickly to the touch of the blackest hand . . . as to the whitest hand." He advised blacks, "The South is the best place for the Negro to work out his salvation."[14]

He even attempted to smooth over the issue of social injus- tice in the southland. He alluded to the fact that racial hostil- ities and social inequality existed in all parts of the country. Washington maintained that the economic arena governed all else, and there blacks and whites could work in harmony be- cause of mutual self-interest. Rights, he said, would follow later as blacks raised themselves to greater economic import- ance. Consequently, in speaking to both whites and blacks, Booker Washington advocated economic fellowship and down- played social and civil rights.

> We may sometimes complain about our not being
> privileged to be housed in certain hotels or about
> being refused the same consideration in restaurants
> as others, but, my friends, the average man of my
> race, perhaps the average man of any race, spends
> a very little part of his time in hotels or restaurants.[15]

The real issue, Washington professed, was money: "The op- portunity to earn a dollar in a factory just now is worth infinite- ly more than the opportunity to spend a dollar in an opera house."[16] Take any job, he advised, and work from there. He told whites that blacks were the best and most dependable labor in the world. He told blacks that the proof was left up to them; they must work even harder and through the proof of their superior labor make themselves indispensable to the country. "Patiently, quietly, doggedly, persistently, through summer and winter, sunshine and shadow, by self-sacrifice, by honesty and industry, we must re-enforce argument with results."[17]

Booker Washington pleaded that blacks be given the tools to cultivate their economic potential, and the most important tool was the right kind of education. Washington frowned upon black intellectualism, or what he considered to be a tendency among blacks to seek education for its own sake.

> We wanted books, more books. The larger the books were the better we liked them. The more the books cost the better we liked them. We did not think much, as a race, about what was in the books; but we thought the mere possession and mere handling and the mere worship of books was going, in some inexplicable way, to make great and strong and useful men of our race. Gradually that old idea has passed away.[18]

If education for blacks was to be meaningful, Washington believed, it must prove to be economically worthwhile to whites.

> The negro teacher and the educated negro must show by the results of education that it does pay to educate the negro. In proportion as the white man sees that the educated, *skilled* [?] [italics mine] negro is worth more to the community than the idle, shiftless negro, in the same degree will the negro make greater progress in the future than in the past, be of more value to himself and of more value to his white neighbors.[19]

This solution, according to him, found its clearest expression in the industrial education initiated at Hampton Institute under Samuel Chapman Armstrong.

Like his mentor, Booker Washington preached the superiority of industrial schooling over that of academic. Although he believed that some blacks should, indeed, be trained in the arts and the professions, he considered this type of education inappropriate and inadvisable for the race as a whole and, moreover, out of the financial reach of most blacks. According to Washington, it took money to engage in the leisure of intellectual exchange. Therefore, industrial success had to come first.

> In the words of the late beloved Frederick Douglass: 'Every blow of the sledge hammer wielded by a sable arm is a powerful blow in support of our cause. Every colored mechanic is by virtue of circumstances an elevator of his race. Every house built by a black man is a strong tower against the allied hosts of prejudice. It is impossible for us to attach too much importance to this aspect of the subject. Without industrial development there can be no wealth; without wealth there can be no leisure; without leisure no opportunity for thoughtful reflection and the cultivation of the higher arts.'[20]

At Tuskegee Institute, Washington strove to instill his students with those attributes that, according to him, would make them essential to the greater prosperity of the country.

> I would set no limits to the attainments of the Negro in arts, in letters or statesmanship, but I believe the surest way to teach those ends is by laying the foundation in the little things of life that lie immediately about one's door. I plead for industrial education and development for the Negro not because I want to cramp him, but because I want to free him. I want to see him enter the all-powerful business and commercial world.[21]

Washington aimed to develop much more than a school. His idea was to make institute, home, and community a cohesive part of Tuskegee Institute. The industrial education idea in his hands became a school-community movement. "An industrial atmosphere pervades the place," one observer noted, "and its air is more that of an industrial community than that of the conventional school. There is something of the hustle and bustle of the business world."[22]

Like the good overseer, and like his mentor, Samuel Chapman Armstrong, Booker T. sought to make his students superb laborers, that is, totally reliable. He criticized Tuskegee students who showed any signs of being unreliable. "Young men come here [Tuskegee Institute] and want to work at this industry or that, for a while, and then get tired and want to change to something else." To be a good worker, Washington professed, one must understand "the Importance of Being Reliable."[23]

Booker Washington worked diligently to please the dominant white society, to make his blacks "the best labor in the world." He watched his students' every move. He was a stickler for precision and detail. The Founder emphasized such things to the Tuskegee student body and teachers as the proper positioning of brooms. Washington sent a notice to three department heads: "Will you kindly see that all brooms in your department are kept on their proper end. I notice that this is not done now." One faculty member responded on top of the Founder's memo: "This must be a mistake."[24] It was not. Booker Washington demanded that everyone, including Mrs. Washington, place and store brooms with the brush end up.[25]

The Founder placed every aspect of the student's life at Tuskegee under a strict regime of rules and regulations. Committees were formed that conducted daily examinations of the students' rooms and personal belongings. Careful attention was given to whether or not all had toothbrushes. One committee reported that it had noted some "absence of tooth brushes and tooth mugs."[26] The Founder received other reports on the toothbrush situation. "There is a very large number of students that use the tooth brush only to adorn the washstand," one of Washington's student informers reported.[27]

The slightest trace of dirt or grime was call for alarm and disciplinary action at Tuskegee. A committee appointed to inspect one of the dorms noted, "The wood work needs scrubbing and dusting thoroughly."[28] The committee also reported that beds were not properly made in military fashion and some of the linen needed ironing and was improperly folded. Students who left their beds unmade were often punished by not receiving dinner.[29]

When Tuskegee students did dine, they did so under stringent rules and regulations. Talking during meals was permitted only at precise intervals designated by the ringing of bells. In 1913 the administration published a formal list of "Rules for Students in the Dining Hall" which read:

1. Remain standing when entering dining room until bell rings for you to sit down.
2. Do not speak to anyone until Grace is sung. All must help sing Grace.
3. Each table must provide proper decorations.
4. You are to have a napkin at each meal and use it.
5. Cut your food up with the knife, convey it to the mouth with the fork, holding same in right hand.
6. Eat all food placed upon your plate.
7. Sit up straight at the table. Do not allow your arms to rest upon table.
8. Do not talk across the aisles. Do not leave the room unexcused.
9. No food is to be wasted upon the table cloth.
10. Report all complaints to stewards or matrons.
11. Regard bells for talking.
12. First bell signal to stop talking.
13. Second bell to get quiet.
14. Students must report to meals on time or be closed out for that meal.[30]

The list of regulations ended with Rule Number 15: "For the violation of the above rules you will be severely punished."[31]

Naturally, students sometimes fell short of the mark. Captain Austin, a stickler for detail, noted that student discipline during meals needed improvement. And no detail escaped his military eye: "Students continue to eat after bell rings and this together with the noise made by the knives and forks tinkling against the plates make it very difficult to hear the adjutant read the notices." In Austin's report to Booker Washington, which contained dining violations, he stated that the men students had become "careless in dress." He complained also about the behavior of women students in the dining hall. "The girls," Austin reported, "are exceedingly boisterous and rough when rising from their tables."[32]

Search and seizure comprised part of the everyday life at Tuskegee. Men and women alike were searched for liquor, obscene materials, or anything else that in some way might contribute to the breakdown of rules or affect the school's "reputation." Searching of students' rooms and personal belongings became official policy at Tuskegee in 1906, when it was written into the School Code.[33]

Booker Washington gave the students' social life the closest scrutiny. The institute forbade male and female students from associating after classes. The woman students received constant reminders from the Dean of Women to remain "moral and pure." This same advice was given to the men students by the Commandant of Cadets. Separate walkways across campus were designated for male and female to guarantee the two kept separated. Male students were forbidden to walk around or near the girls' dormitory after dusk. This was done, as one school official put it, to "prevent the promiscuous mingling of boys and girls."[34]

Washington was working to make Tuskegee students into the type of blacks that the white South relished. Their training was primarily in "how to behave" rather than in how to become skilled tradesmen. To be a skilled craftsman requires proficiency in mathematical and verbal skills. The school's curriculum, however, was industrial almost to the total exclusion of the academic. What academic studies that did exist were secondary and often optional.[35] That the school would commit itself to this type of program was clear from the staff that Washington employed at the school. Most of the faculty members were Hampton graduates, and they knew more about discipline than trades.[36]

The *Southern Workman* reported that Hampton graduates held most of the key posts at Tuskegee Institute, noting the fact that the school's principal was "Hampton's most distinguished graduate."[37] Washington issued a directive in 1908 to his departmental heads in which he stated that he wanted the school to "employ each year a reasonable number of Hampton graduates." He added that he "did not want the number of Hampton graduates decreased on the teaching force at Tuskegee."[38]

The Founder was not completely closeminded in hiring personnel for teaching positions at Tuskegee, but instructors he hired from academic institutions often failed to fit well into his educational scheme because he subordinated every aspect of Tuskegee's educational program to the industrial schooling idea of producing tractable blacks. Blacks from academic universities like Howard, Fisk, and Atlanta were employed at the school. Roscoe Conkling Bruce, a product of Harvard University who headed the so-called academic curriculum at Tuskegee, found that the institute's commitment to preparing students as common laborers was total. Bruce thought that perhaps some of the students might be material for professional careers. He complained about educating students "chiefly in accordance with the demands for labor."[39]

Another thorn in Washington's side was a young instructor in the academic department named Leslie P. Hill, who had been hired by Bruce. Hill obviously failed to adjust to the second-class status of academic studies at Tuskegee. He initiated innovative approaches to his teaching of educational theory, history, and philosophy. However, the Founder regarded Hill as hostile to the educational philosophy of the school. Washington, in his explanation for firing Hill, remarked that the young Harvard graduate seemed to feel that the methods employed at Tuskegee were "either wrong or dangerous."[40]

If he had many of the school's instructors in mind, Hill was absolutely right. Higher education at Tuskegee was a sad joke. Hill recognized that the general atmosphere discouraged serious effort among the industrial faculty. He noted that courses lacked outlines, instructors failed to use facilities properly, and that many of them lacked the competence to teach the skills for which they were hired.[41]

Roscoe Bruce found the entire Tuskegee situation quite perplexing. He understood that Tuskegee was an industrial school —a fact, Bruce remarked, that he was "often reminded of." But he said that he failed to see how students who received little to no academic training would be able to carry on up-to-date craft positions. He wrote to the principal, "You see, the truth is that the carpenter is not taught enough mathematics, the machinist enough physics, or the farmer enough chemistry for the purpose of his particular work." Bruce also found it discouraging that there was no distinction made in the school's curriculum between those students who were going to be teachers and the ones "who plan to make horseshoes or to paint houses."[42]

Washington conceded that some difficulties existed with the industrial idea of education, but that he had said so in his book, *Up From Slavery.*

> I told those who doubted the wisdom of the plan [industrial education] that I knew our first buildings would not be so comfortable or so complete in their finish as buildings erected by the experienced hands of outside workmen, but that in the teaching of civilization, self-help, and self-reliance, the erection of the buildings by the students themselves would more than compensate for any lack of comfort or fine finish.[43]

His point, no doubt, was that problems are to be expected but they will be solved in time.

Regardless of what Booker T. said, Tuskegee was not preparing its students to take their place as skilled artisans in the industrial world. The school maintained a general policy of allowing students to graduate without even having finished a trade course. One report indicated that some positions calling for manual skills had become open to blacks in the South and that the opportunities for the Tuskegee graduates were "greater than ever," but that the students were not properly prepared for these jobs.[44]

Roscoe C. Bruce reported to Washington on another separate occasion in which he complained that upon visiting the Girls'

Laundry Department he was struck by the lack of any real skills training. Bruce said that the students did not seem to be receiving instruction in the art of the task but in fact simply performed menial chores.[45]

W.T.B. Williams of the General Education Board conducted a survey of Tuskegee in 1906 and concluded that the student who completed the course of studies had what might be equivalent to a ninth grade education in the public school system. He considered there to be a general lack of training and preparation at the school. In addition, said Williams, "the majority of the students are barely able to read the Bible." He said in conclusion, "Considering the elementary nature of much of this work and the maturity of the students, the daily requirements seem pretty light."[46]

The lack of quality in instruction and academic training at Tuskegee drove Roscoe Bruce to resign in 1906. Washington replaced him with J.R.E. Lee, who fit well into the Tuskegee idea. But Lee's own correspondence reveals the lack of serious academic or skills education at the school. Lee noted that the students who had attended one or two years of education at the general education schools, such as Fisk or Atlanta, were able to go immediately to the senior ranks at Tuskegee. Lee admitted that the work required of students at those schools was "far above the work required here [at Tuskegee]."[47]

The lack of a positive, achievement-oriented atmosphere at Tuskegee had a negative effect on students and teachers. In 1912, one Tuskegee instructor openly admitted that the students they produced were ill-equipped to pursue a skilled occupation in industry. He thought that perhaps the problem lay with the teachers. He begged that they "give more time and attention" to their duties.[48]

Instructors, on the other hand, blamed the problem on the students. Teachers in the industrial classes claimed that the students lacked the necessary attitude to become tradesmen, that they took their assignments lightly and performed them poorly. The instructor in basic construction and design accused the students of not following floor plans and of being sloppy and lazy in the performance of their tasks.[49]

However, the teachers seemed more preoccupied with social matters than with correcting their students' deficiencies. "The young women teachers engage in frivolities hardly in keeping with their calling," W.T.B. Williams reported. "They are good women but not seriously concerned about the work in hand. They seem to give far more attention to dress rather than to almost anything else. . . ."[50]

The female instructors were not alone. The men could stand on their own in terms of being frivolous. They repeatedly hosted gala social outings. One example was the going away party for Booker T. Washington, Jr., given in his honor by the faculty men. It was an elaborate and extravagant affair with orchestra, "seating arrangements patterned after that in the Cabinet Room of the White House," and dinner crowned with "Fried Chicken, Booker T. Washington, Jr. Style."[51]

After a visit to Tuskegee in 1904, Robert Curtis Ogden commented on the "peculiar" social attitude of the school's faculty. He and his other white companions had been guests of honor at a faculty-hosted concert of classical music. Ogden, commenting later to Booker Washington about the concert, said that he believed his guests appreciated the entertainment, but that they would have enjoyed seeing more of the teachers and students at work rather than watching their hosts do their "level best to be like white folks and not natural."[52]

Tuskegee's faculty was imitative of whites, but they were black and not the omnipotent authority symbol that, for example, Hampton's all-white staff was to its students. Tuskegee students, justifiably, found faults with the faculty, the education they received, and the conditions of campus life. They voiced their displeasure. The class in agricultural science at Tuskegee was taught by the renowned George Washington Carver, and he could not escape the growing discontent among students. One student complained that he had come to Tuskegee to learn the most advanced techniques in farming from George Washington Carver but found that the professor seemed to be more interested in producing "hired hands." The student remarked that overall he felt that he was "not receiving progressive instruction."[53]

In addition, students challenged the strict discipline of the school in subtle ways. Julio Despaigne, Washington's key informant in the dorms, reported, "The students have the habit of making their beds at the morning good for when the inspector comes that he can find it well, and in the afternoon they disorder them and put clean and dirty clothes on them."[54]

The rebellion of the students against the oppressive social restrictions of the institute manifested itself in different subtle ways. Some students began skipping chapel to meet with members of the opposite sex.[55] Others volunteered for duties that held a high likelihood of putting them in contact with the opposite sex; a favorite assignment among male and female students was night duty at the school's hospital. Those fortunate enough to draw that duty were on their honor not to fraternize. The administration, however, soon found out the hospital was being used as a place for social carousing. Walter McFadden and Katie Paterson received an official reprimand from the administration "for questionable socializing while on night duty together at the hospital."[56]

Some male students placed latches on their doors to keep night inspectors from entering while they, allegedly, broke school rules. This was met with quick action on the part of the administration. The Executive Council decided that because of

> the misconduct, gambling and so forth, which is indulged in on the part of certain young men who place night latches on their doors and lock themselves into their rooms from teachers' and officers' attempts to get into the room and who jump out of the windows before they can be detected in their mischief: because of this it has been found necessary to remove all the night latches from the doors.[57]

The women students of the laundry class asserted themselves against unfair practices. They could not understand why they should be paid less than their labor was worth. They objected to the hard work with low pay. The young women said that they had the work of both students and teachers to do including that of the summer teachers and that on one occasion they

had remained until five o'clock on Saturday evening in order
to supply the boys with their week's laundry. "We hope you
will not think of us as complainers," they closed in their letter
to Booker Washington, "but, simply as children striving to perform their duty; and, at the same time receive some recompense
in return. We are asking for higher wages. May we have it?"[58]
The Founder's answer was to appoint a committee to investigate
their complaint, with the quiet result that nothing ever came
of it.

The students' discontent gradually gave way to outright hostility against the school. Students stole from the institution,
broke windows, wrecked dormitories, defaced walls, and on
several occasions debased the school chapel.[59] Some tried to
avoid school and work by pretending to be ill. The institute's
physician reported to Booker Washington, "I wish you also to
bear in mind that a large number of the students who come to
the hospital are not calling because they are ill, but are simply
giving way to some imaginary ills, or else taking advantage of
the easy method of losing an hour or two from work."[60] One
student spoke bluntly to Washington about the feeling among
many of the students that to be successful at the school it was
required to become "slaves of you [Mr. Washington] and Tuskegee."[61] A group of native-born African students, accused of
challenging the authority of one of their instructors and later
brought before Washington for discipline, criticized the education they were receiving at Tuskegee and the attitude of teachers, including the Founder himself, who they said "acted as a
master ordering his slaves." They concluded: "We do not intend
no longer to remain in your institution. . . ."[62]

Students openly rebelled against the school's disciplinary
practices. Charles H. Washington, a member of the senior class,
considered the prying eyes of the faculty into every aspect of
the individual student's private life to be too much for him. He
told a faculty member point-blank to pass on the word that
they "are to cease meddling with his affairs."[63]

During the last ten years of Washington's reign at Tuskegee,
from 1905 to his death in 1915, faculty members alluded to a
growing student hostility against them. They became fearful
for their personal safety, believing that students were carrying

weapons and ready to use them. The situation at Tuskegee became more tense with the passing of each day. Students acted discourteously to instructors in and out of class. A group of faculty members reported to Washington that pupils had become so rebellious that they "never felt safe in appearing before the students."[64]

In the tradition of the overseer whose position is dependent upon his ability to keep those under his charge in line, Washington met student discontent each step of the way with a tightening of rules and regulations. But student unrest continued. The result was that discipline at Tuskegee during the latter part of his administration approached absurdity. Students were suspended for talking without permission, failing to dress according to standards, or even for "failing to take a napkin to the dining hall."[65] Young men students were chastised for "putting their hands in their pockets," and failing to obey that rule, the administration sought to offer "such inducements as will make them do so."[66]

That the punishment students received outweighed the offense is clearly indicated in the case of Lewis Smith, whom a fellow student accused of "over indiscrete conduct with Emma Penny of the same class." Smith, a senior and slated to graduate as class salutatorian, was brought before the administration for allegedly attempting to hug and kiss Miss Penny. Although he denied the charges and his testimony was substantiated by a fellow classmate, the administration saw fit to punish Smith. He was denied the distinction of graduating as class salutatorian.[67]

Smith was lucky. He could have been suspended or expelled —favorite disciplinary measures during the latter years of Booker T.'s rule over Tuskegee Institute. A case in point is the 1912 flag incident. A few members of the senior class of that year decided to celebrate by flying their class flag over Tompkins Hall. They made the unpardonable mistake, however, of not obtaining the administration's permission. School officials considered the students' act a conspiracy against the institute's authority, an "organized movement on the part of some of the members of the senior class . . . and that this was not carried out on the spur of the moment."[68] The accused students begged for mercy and swore that they acted out of no intent to challenge school authority or embarrass the administration. One of the accused vowed they would rather have had their "heads severed from their bodies" than to do anything against Tuskegee. The young men were suspended.[69]

The slightest infraction on the part of the student, or even suspicion of having broken a rule, was reason enough for the Washington administration to notify parents. This had near disastrous results in the case of Charles Bell, a senior who was brought before the administration on the suspicion of having engaged in "sexual misconduct" with a young woman named Varner of the same class. Both denied the charges. There was no eyewitness testimony or other "proof" that Bell and Varner had done anything wrong, except the fact that they were often seen together. The administration, nevertheless, passed its suspicions on to Miss Varner's father. He showed up later on campus with his gun, saying that he would shoot Bell on sight. Bell was forced to leave the institute until the situation quieted.[70]

When Tuskegee students did pose a real threat to the sovereignty of Booker Washington, he showed no mercy. In 1903, a group of Tuskegee students launched a strike against the school. The material on the strike, and it is extremely sketchy, does indicate that the participants objected to the entire Tuskegee order of things. They wanted more academic training, better instruction, more opportunity to learn trades, and an easing of rules and regulations. Washington's response was undiluted: "No concessions."[71]

In an official but insubstantial report on the strike to the school's white financial backers, Booker T. contended that a few malcontents had occupied one of the school's buildings, thinking that this was the way to be heard. The students were not upset with the institute, he said, "nor were they in opposition to any industrial work," but "objected to being required to devote too much time to both industrial work and studies with too little time for preparation." The strike apparently ended as quickly as it had begun once the administration served notice that all those who failed to return to work immediately would be expelled.[72]

Those who obtained an "education" at Tuskegee did so in accordance with the industrial schooling idea and under the watchful eyes of Booker Taliaferro Washington. Student dissatisfaction did nothing to change the Founder's mind about the rightness of the type of educational philosophy he professed and protected. His administration practiced a stiff brand of discipline that it never backed down from. But students, on occasion, continued to try and voice their complaints. Perhaps it is understandable, then, why the Washington administration felt it might be necessary to establish a "guard house" for the purpose of confining its student incorrigibles. It did just that in 1912.[73]

Booker T.'s educational practices were based on his desire to please whites and gain their support. The Founder worked to make whites more a part of the school's operations. He invited them to visit the institute on every occasion. He believed that the school's annual commencement exercises afforded an excellent opportunity to win goodwill from the local whites. "I think it would be well for you to spend a week in Montgomery among the white and colored people," Washington advised a fellow faculty member. "I am very anxious that in addition to the colored people we have a large representative class of whites to attend Commencement."[74] In fact, the Founder considered paying the fares of white visitors to the commencement exercises.[75] The school advertised the commencement of 1904 in the *Tuskegee News.*[76]

Washington did everything possible to bring in more local white support. When Washington received advice from a "reliable source" that if he kept the number of Jews down in attendance at commencement, more local whites would probably come, he responded: "Of course I do not want to keep the Jews away, but I think it would be a good plan to increase the number of Gentiles if possible."[77]

The Founder received unsolicited advice on how to gain more local and national support. One Northerner wrote him suggesting that the school would gain more support if it devoted itself exclusively to the production of domestic servants. The writer suggested that the program should stress "cooking, waiting on table, cleaning silver and washing windows, sewing, dusting, washing and ironing."[78]

In his response, Washington made it clear that Tuskegee did this and more:

> At this institution we give training in every line of domestic work, hence any girl who finishes our course should be able to perform any of the usual duties connected with a servant's life, but one of the most important things to be accomplished for the colored people now is the getting of them to have correct ideas concerning labor, that is to get them to feel that all classes of labor, whether of the head or hand, are dignified. This lesson I think Tuskegee, in connection with Hampton, has been successful in teaching the race.[79]

And, like Hampton, Tuskegee aimed to do more than serve as an agency to place individual domestics. Washington in conclusion said that the most economical thing to be done was to send out a set of people not only trained in hand but thoroughly equipped in mind and heart so that they themselves could go out and start smaller centers or training schools. He believed that it would be of greater service to the whole country "if we can train at Tuskegee one girl who could go out and start a domestic training school in Atlanta, Baltimore, or elsewhere, than we would be doing by trying to put servants directly into individual houses which would be a never ending task."[80]

But no matter what advice he did follow, Washington and Tuskegee did not gain the full support of the white South during his lifetime. As was the case with the black overseer in the antebellum South, there were those who would never believe that a black could be trusted to oversee his fellow blacks to the best interests of whites. In *Up From Slavery*, Washington grossly misstated the white response to his educational efforts in Macon County when he wrote that the "Tuskegee school at the present time has no warmer and more enthusiastic friends anywhere than it has among the white citizens of Tuskegee and throughout the state of Alabama and the entire South."[81] The evidence suggests a different interpretation. One of the area's white residents wrote a critical interpretation of Tuskegee Institute, which he said was shared by many white Southerners. The author claimed that after careful examination, it was clear to him that Booker Washington was misleading people to think that Tuskegee was a harmless institution. He contended that Washington wanted racial and social equality and that he worked forcefully for it.[82]

Clearer evidence of the lack of Southern support for Tuskegee Institute was given by Monroe Work in 1910. Work reported that the 2,980 pledged Southern white supporters had that year given to the institute a grand total of $73.20.[83] With this type of Southern support it is little wonder that Washington looked elsewhere for the school's bread and butter. The soliciting of funds, however, necessitated that he spend a great deal of his time on speaking tours in the North. "Nearly one-half of my time," he estimated, "is spent away from Tuskegee, addressing audiences. . . ."[84] It was this type of exposure that made him the most prominent black person in America.

But Booker T. faced the dilemma of the loyal "darkie," who no matter how faithfully and well he acted was still the wrong color. Although most Southern whites found solace in Washington's accommodating tone, his acceptance of black political and civil inequality, and his work at Tuskegee, they would not help a black man become prominent even if that prominence was a direct result of his contribution to the status quo. The attitude of the average Southerner to the prestige Washington had acquired since his famed Atlanta Exposition address in 1895 ran from critical to hostile. When Booker T. dined with President Theodore Roosevelt in 1901, many Southerners saw this as a direct contradiction to the utterances he had made in his Atlanta address supporting social inequality. One Southern white man wrote to the Founder telling him that it would be best if he stayed in the South and turned down invitations to socialize with whites. Other advice was more direct. Washington confided later that the dinner with the president had put his life in jeopardy.[85]

Washington found himself in deep trouble four years later when he accepted an invitation to dine with the retail store magnate, John Wanamaker, and his daughter at the United

States Hotel in New York. Articles appearing throughout the Southern press were critical of Booker T.'s social outings. Washington's life was again in jeopardy. His train route back to Tuskegee had to be kept secret for fear that some whites might mob the Founder. Before leaving New York, Booker Washington received a wire from his secretary, Emmett Scott, in Tuskegee. Scott advised him to make himself as inconspicuous as possible and keep his train schedule secret. To this he added: "I think that you can come to Tuskegee without delay, taking of course, the precautions I have already mentioned en route. If there is any trouble, it is more likely to manifest itself on the train. . . ."[86]

Booker T. Washington never intentionally did anything to upset or anger Southern whites. He repledged his love for the South and his obedience to its traditions in *My Larger Education*, published four years before his death. The Founder said in that work, "I understand thoroughly the prejudices, the customs, the traditions of the South—and, strange as it may seem to those who do not wholly understand the situation, I love the South."[87] The philosophy of "uplift" for blacks that he preached across the nation and taught at Tuskegee Institute was in accordance with that love and the prevailing racial, economic order. His role was like that of the black overseer during slavery who, given the position of authority over his fellow slaves, worked diligently to keep intact the very system under which they both were enslaved.

NOTES

1. Paulo Freire, *Pedagogy of the Oppressed* (New York: Herder and Herder, 1972; translated from the original Portuguese manuscript, by Myra B. Ramos, 1968), p. 55.

2. For discussion along this line see Sidney M. Willhelm, *Who Needs the Negro?* (New York: Doubleday, 1971), pp. 64-66, 288.

3. Rayford W. Logan, *The Betrayal of the Negro* (London: Collier Books, 1969), originally published as *The Negro in American Life and Thought: The Nadir, 1877-1901*, 1965. For further discussion see Richard Hofstadter's classic study, *Social Darwinism in American Thought* (Boston: Beacon Press, 1955), first published by University of Pennsylvania Press, 1944.

4. Archibald H. Grimke, "Why Disfranchisement Is Bad," *Atlantic Monthly* (July 1904), pp. 72-74; Kelly Miller, "Social Equality," *National Magazine* (February 1905), p. 6.

5. Miller, "Social Equality," p. 6.

6. Booker T. Washington, "Address Before the National Unitarian Association at Saratoga, New York" (26 September 1896), *Booker T. Washington Papers*, Library of Congress.

7. Booker T. Washington, "The South as an Opening for a Business Career," Address Delivered at Lincoln University (26 April 1888), *Booker T. Washington Papers*.

8. Booker T. Washington, "Address Delivered at Raleigh, North Carolina" (30 October 1903), *Booker T. Washington Papers*.

9. Booker T. Washington, "The South as an Opening for a Business Career" (26 April 1888), *Booker T. Washington Papers*.

10. Booker T. Washington, "Address Delivered at Raleigh, North Carolina" (30 October 1903), *Booker T. Washington Papers*.

11. Booker T. Washington, "The Progress of the Negro," Address Delivered at a Meeting of the New York Congregational Club (16 January 1893), *Booker T. Washington Papers*.

12. Booker T. Washington, "Some Results of The Armstrong Idea," Address Delivered at Hampton Institute, in Celebration of Founder's Day (31 January 1909), p. 11, *Armstrong Family Papers*, Williams College.

13. Ibid., p. 10.

14. Ibid., pp. 5, 4.

15. Ibid., p. 5.

16. Booker T. Washington, "Atlanta Exposition Speech" (1895), *Booker T. Washington Papers*.

17. Cited in William Loren Katz, ed., *The Negro Problem* (New York: Arno Press, 1969), p. 28.

18. Washington, "Some Results of The Armstrong Idea," p. 8.

19. "Booker Washington Outlines Negro's Duty in Materializing South's Industrial Destiny," *Atlanta Constitution*, 5 February 1911, p. 12.

20. Cited in Katz, pp. 18-19.

21. Ibid., p. 19.

22. W.T.B. Williams, "Tuskegee Institute, Confidential Report to Members of the General Education Board" (1906), *Booker T. Washington Papers*.

23. Booker T. Washington, *Character Building* (New York: Doubleday, 1902), p. 107.

24. Booker T. Washington to P. C. Parks, E. J. Scott, and C. H. Gibson, 11 November 1904, *Booker T. Washington Papers*.

25. Ibid.

26. Committee to Inspect Phelps Hall to Booker T. Washington, 22 October 1904, *Booker T. Washington Papers.*

27. Julio Despaigne to Booker T. Washington, 22 September 1905, *Booker T. Washington Papers.*

28. Committee to Inspect Phelps Hall to Booker T. Washington, 22 October 1904.

29. "Minutes of the Executive Council" (15 September 1904), *Booker T. Washington Papers.*

30. "Rules for Students in the Dining Hall" (1913), *Booker T. Washington Papers.*

31. Ibid.

32. Captain George Austin to Booker T. Washington, 1906, *Booker T. Washington Papers.*

33. Booker T. Washington to Miss Jane Clark, 1 June 1906, *Booker T. Washington Papers.*

34. S. Helen Porter and Major Julius B. Ramsey to Executive Council, 17 March 1910, *Booker T. Washington Papers.*

35. Monroe N. Work to Booker T. Washington, 28 May 1910, *Booker T. Washington Papers.*

36. For a discussion see Chapter 2.

37. "Hampton at Tuskegee," *Southern Workman* (October 1915), p. 537.

38. "Minutes of the Executive Council" (3 June 1908), *Booker T. Washington Papers.*

39. Roscoe C. Bruce to Booker T. Washington, 12 April 1906, *Booker T. Washington Papers.*

40. Booker T. Washington, *My Larger Education* (New York: Doubleday, Page & Co., 1911), pp. 129-130; Booker T. Washington to Leslie P. Hill, 21 May 1906, *Booker T. Washington Papers.*

41. Edward T. Attwell to Booker T. Washington, 9 February 1907, *Booker T. Washington Papers.*

42. Roscoe C. Bruce to Booker T. Washington, 12 April 1906, *Booker T. Washington Papers.*

43. Booker T. Washington, *Up From Slavery* (New York: Doubleday, 1901), pp. 148-149.

44. Monroe N. Work, "Report of a Study of Tuskegee Students Made to the Trustees of the Tuskegee Normal and Industrial Institute" (10 June 1910), *Booker T. Washington Papers.* Work concluded that Tuskegee was "an Industrial school, but for the most part not a vocational school." [Monroe N. Work to Booker T. Washington, 29 December 1910, *Booker T. Washington Papers.*] A student in the landscaping class complained to the Founder, "I have been on this division about ten months and have

never had any instruction. . . . And many other things we should be told how to do and what we do it for." [James R. Broddus to Booker T. Washington, 7 February 1904, *Booker T. Washington Papers.*]

45. Roscoe C. Bruce to Booker T. Washington, 29 December 1903, *Booker T. Washington Papers.*

46. W.T.B. Williams, "Tuskegee Institute, Confidential Report to Members of the General Education Board" (May 1906), p. 3, *Booker T. Washington Papers.*

47. "Minutes of the Faculty" (16 September 1910), *Booker T. Washington Papers.*

48. Ibid., 6 December 1912.

49. Lloyd G. Wheeler to Booker T. Washington, 14 May 1908, *Booker T. Washington Papers.*

50. Williams, "Tuskegee Institute," p. 37.

51. "Entertaining Mr. Washington, Jr.," *Tuskegee Student* (26 September 1908).

52. Roscoe Bruce to R. R. Taylor, 3 May 1904, *Booker T. Washington Papers.*

53. Booker T. Washington to George W. Carver, 5 March 1905, *Booker T. Washington Papers.*

54. Julio Despaigne to Booker T. Washington, 22 September 1905, *Booker T. Washington Papers.*

55. S. Helen Porter to Booker T. Washington, 12 April 1912, *Booker T. Washington Papers.*

56. Dr. James A. Kenney to Executive Council, 18 November 1904, *Booker T. Washington Papers.*

57. "Minutes of the Executive Council" (26 March 1914), *Booker T. Washington Papers.*

58. Laundry Girls to Booker T. Washington, 12 July 1911, Special Committee to Booker T. Washington, 15 July 1911, *Booker T. Washington Papers.*

59. Edward T. Attwell to James A. Bailey, 23 July 1908, Julio Despaigne to Booker T. Washington, 22 September 1905, *Booker T. Washington Papers.*

60. Dr. James A. Kenney to Executive Council, 6 December 1909, *Booker T. Washington Papers.*

61. Julio Despaigne to Booker T. Washington, 22 September 1905, *Booker T. Washington Papers.*

62. "Memo," Booker T. Washington, 5 March 1904, *Booker T. Washington Papers.*

63. Captain Austin to Booker Washington, 21 September 1904, *Booker T. Washington Papers.*

64. "Minutes of the Faculty" (15 January 1913), *Booker T. Washington Papers.*

65. S. Helen Porter to Executive Council, 29 September 1910, *Booker T. Washington Papers.*

66. Major Ramsey to Executive Council, 6 March 1911, *Booker T. Washington Papers.*

67. "Minutes of the Executive Council" (10 May 1898), *Booker T. Washington Papers.*

68. "Report of the Committee to Investigate Flag Raising" (4 January 1912), *Booker T. Washington Papers.*

69. Seniors to Booker T. Washington, 2 January 1912, *Booker T. Washington Papers.*

70. James H. Washington to Booker Washington, 24 September 1888, *Booker T. Washington Papers.*

71. "Minutes of the Executive Council" (27 September 1903), *Booker T. Washington Papers.*

72. Booker T. Washington to William H. Baldwin, Jr., 23 October 1903, *Booker T. Washington Papers.*

73. Major Ramsey to Booker T. Washington, 17 May 1912, Booker Washington to Major Ramsey, 17 May 1912, *Booker T. Washington Papers.*

74. Booker Washington to Calvin Calloway, 3 May 1904, *Booker T. Washington Papers.*

75. Booker Washington to Edward T. Attwell, 1 May 1909, *Booker T. Washington Papers.*

76. Ibid., 2 May 1909.

77. Ibid.

78. Mrs. Arthur Gilman to Booker T. Washington, 6 May 1907, *Booker T. Washington Papers.*

79. Booker T. Washington to Mrs. Arthur Gilman, 15 May 1907, *Booker T. Washington Papers.*

80. Ibid.

81. Washington, *Up From Slavery*, pp. 136-137.

82. Stanton Becker von Greybil, *Letters from Tuskegee: Being the Confessions of a Yankee* (Alabama: Roberts, 1905).

83. Booker T. Washington, *The Story of My Life* (Atlanta: Nichols, 1900), p. 214.

84. Monroe Work to Booker T. Washington, 16 July 1914, *Booker T. Washington Papers.*

85. Anson Phelps Stokes, *A Brief Biography of Booker T. Washington* (Hampton, Va.: Hampton Institute Press, 1936), pp. 29-30.

86. Emmett Jay Scott to Booker T. Washington, 7 September 1905, *Booker T. Washington Papers.*

87. Washington, *My Larger Education*, p. 180.

4

CRUSADERS FOR SERVITUDE: THE INDUSTRIAL EDUCATION MOVEMENT

"Negro labor would never become excited by impossible ambition unless the spirit of unrest were stirred within him by education for which he was unfitted," Booker T. Washington declared in 1896.[1] These words must have rung with delight in the ears of Northern industrialists who had economic interests in the South. Northern money dominated the development of industry in the New South, and the captains of those industrial enterprises became acutely aware of the value of black labor. Industrial education would aid in the heightened exploitation of that labor. It is little wonder, then, that a movement in support of industrial schooling would gain the support of Northern industrial magnates. Thus, the crusade for industrial education in the South became a rallying point for the exploiters of black labor.

The end of the Civil War marked the triumph of Northern capitalism over Southern capitalism. Northern capital moved steadily into the South after the war, and many Southern industries and resources became Northern prizes. Railroads were an inviting frontier. One result of the war was the destruction of Southern railroads. Rebuilding and further expansion commenced during Reconstruction. In the vast majority of cases, Southern railroads were Southern in name only. Most railroads in the South were run on Northern capital. Georgia's lines, for example, were under the control of Northern investors. Stocks in the Central Railroad of Georgia were sold in the North. The

Macon and Western was under the control of Northern firms, represented by Morris K. Jesup.[2] Jesup also served as general agent for the Macon and Brunswick lines. A powerful railroad magnate by the end of the Civil War, he maintained controlling interest in the Wilmington and Manchester Railroad of North Carolina in addition to his control over various Georgia lines. Morris K. Jesup became known as the man in charge of Southern railroad bonds. He was a permanent fixture on Wall Street. Jesup sold bonds and stock in the Montgomery and Eufaula, Macon and Augusta, Atlantic and Gulf, South Georgia, Florida, and many other lines. There was an old saying around Wall Street that "if it ran on two rails and was located in the South and you wanted to buy some stock in it, then Morris K. Jesup was the man to see."[3]

Railroad mergers and the movement of Northern capital into Southern railroads increased rapidly after the Panic of 1873. In 1874, there was formed one of the most efficient railroad pools in the United States, the Southern Railway and Steamship Company. The SR & SC pooled twenty-two railroads of the South and a smaller number of associated coastal steamers running to Baltimore, Philadelphia, Boston, and New York. During this same period (1874-1876), J. Pierpont Morgan gained control over several formally defunct Georgia and Alabama lines. In 1894, Morgan officially established the Southern Railway and brought in William H. Baldwin, Jr., of New York to serve as vice-president in charge of operation and traffic. It was Baldwin who, in fact, built the Southern Railway. The Southern engaged in the shipping of coal, iron, cotton, lumber, and even fruit. Under Baldwin's ideas for efficiency the Southern soon showed huge profits—a trend that was to continue throughout the twentieth century.[4]

The dominance of Northern capital in the Southern railroad industry continued in the twentieth century. In 1910, for example, the Virginia Railway Company was formed by H. H. Rogers, President of Standard Oil in the South. Rogers, an outstanding Northern businessman, constructed the Virginia Railway with his own capital and that of Northern associates. This vastly profitable railway was totally controlled by Northern capitalists. Rogers was its founder, and the entire Board of Directors was comprised of Northerners, all from New York.[5] Other railroad magnates of the period were Jay Gould, Russell Sage, Collis P. Huntington, Calvin Bruce, William K. Vanderbilt, Andrew Carnegie, and John D. Rockefeller. All of these men had strong economic interests in Southern railroads.

Southern coal, iron, and steel came to be largely under the control of Northern capital, including Virginia's mines and furnaces. The Birmingham *Iron Age* of Alabama declared that scarcely a week passed that capitalists from the North did not invade their city.[6] The largest producer was the Tennessee Coal, Iron and Railroad Company. TCI & R owned enormous reserves of iron ore, coal, dolomite, and lime, which were located within a small region in Northern Alabama and Southern Tennessee. Its iron ore holdings were estimated at 700 million tons, and its coal reserves were larger. Consolidation and mergers brought twelve additional coal and iron companies under TCI & R, including the huge DeBardeleben Company. The United States Steel Corporation, an enterprise of the Northern magnate J. P. Morgan and associates, purchased TCI & R on November 5, 1907.[7]

The vast Southern cotton industry was open for the taking once the Civil War ended, and Northern investors moved in. The *Financial Chronicle* on 23 September 1865 made reference to the fact that the flow of Northern capital to the Southern cotton industry had already begun and was "progressing in a daily increasing current."[8] Two months later the *Chronicle* reported: "Northern capitalists will invest large amounts in the South which will chiefly be devoted to the raising of cotton."[9] Northern investment in Tennessee cotton was so widespread that the *Chronicle* reported on 20 January 1866: "Northern capital is so abundant in Tennessee that it is flowing across the state line for investment in Georgia, Alabama, Mississippi, and even Arkansas."[10] In addition, it was reported that Northern capitalists were migrating southward and many Southern industries were "changing hands."[11]

The flow of Northern capital southward increased at a steady rate. It was discovered that cotton by-products might be profitable. Cottonseed oil became a new frontier. Cottonseeds had traditionally been used as cattle feed, or when left to rot, high-grade fertilizer for Southern agriculture, until it was realized that its by-product, oil, could be refined. The oil could be combined with beef sterine to make "cottonlene," which was a popular substitute for lard, or the oil could be used as a base in the composition of various soaps and washing powders. Northern money soon controlled the cottonseed oil industry. The Amercan Cotton Oil Trust was formed in 1884. This trust was Northern dominated and eventually controlled over 80 percent of the entire crushing capacity in the United States, which numbered some 131 mills, all of which were located in the South. The American Cotton Oil Trust operated similar to the Standard Oil Company and "was of great concern to many of Standard's people."[12] The relationship between the American Cotton Oil Trust and Rockefeller's Standard Oil was more than coincidental. J. H. Flagler, a member of the company, headed the American Cotton Oil Trust. Under Flagler's leadership, ACOT dictated the policies and pooled the profits of the majority of cotton oil mills and associated establishments in the United States.

Black labor had a role in the production of every resource of the South. It was a major source in the building of Southern railroads. Blacks flocked to Louisiana, Texas, Arkansas, and Georgia, where they could be sure of employment on the lines. Morris K. Jesup, for example, was a staunch advocate of black labor in building Georgian railroads. The Morgan-owned and Baldwin-operated Southern Railway was built by black labor. More than 5,000 blacks were used by Baldwin in the building of the Southern Railway.[13] Employers preferred black laborers because of their "immense efficiency, faithfulness and their non-union affiliation."[14] They were readily utilized as common laborers. Most railroad employers shared the common belief that blacks were better suited for the rigors of railroad work. The United States Industrial Commission found that the railroads employed blacks mainly to do the unskilled and heavy work.[15]

Black labor was immensely important to Southern coal. The Tennessee Coal, Iron and Railroad Company maintained the reputation of being the largest single employer of black labor in the South.[16] Several of the TCI & R mines were totally worked by blacks.[17] TCI & R benefited from the tremendous influx of black labor in the Birmingham district during the last quarter of the nineteenth century. In 1870, fewer than 2,500 blacks lived in Jefferson County, and only 5,000 in the district. Thirty years later, 67,000 lived in the Birmingham district, 57,000 of them in Jefferson County and 16,500 of those in Birmingham.[18] In 1880, over 40 percent of the district's four hundred miners were black. By the end of the nineteenth century, blacks made up over 35 percent of the population in that district and even 40 percent in Jefferson County. By the beginning of the twentieth century, 65 percent of the industrial workers in Birmingham were black. The owners were delighted by the increase of available black workers in the district.[19]

In addition to its well-known role in cotton planting and harvesting, it is clear that black labor was a major force for the success in the cotton-oil mills of the South. This was not the case in cotton mills, for white women were often employed there. The employment of blacks in cotton-oil mills increased steadily. The *Tradesman* reported that the industry in Texas, which had the largest number of skilled and semi-skilled black workmen, "is a cotton oil company employing 300 hands. Of these 100 are skilled or semi-skilled. They attend to the machinery used in the manufacture of the oil cake and meal and the like, firing boilers, running presses, etc. . . . and compare favorably in efficiency with the white workman." In the majority of the cotton-oil mills, blacks comprised the bulk of the work force.[20]

A New South was in the making, an emerging, industrial South laced with Northern capital. These were critical years for the African-American. W.E.B. Du Bois wrote of the period that

> for the American Negro, the last decade of the 19th and the first decade of the 20th centuries were more critical than the Reconstruction years of 1868 to 1876. . . . This was the age of triumph for big business, for industry, consolidated and organized on a

world-wide scale, and run by white capital with colored labor. The Southern United States was one of
the most promising fields for this development, with
. . . a mass of cheap and potentially efficient labor.[21]

How best guarantee a stabilized and efficient black labor force?
At Hampton Institute, in Hampton, Virginia, and at Tuskegee
Institute, in Tuskegee, Alabama, an answer was being formu-
lated.

J.L.M. Curry, a former Confederate and pro-slavery congress-
man, was a leading force in articulating that answer. The most
prolific years in his life were between 1881 and 1903, when he
championed the New South Movement. Curry's most important
work, judged Amory D. Mayo, associate editor of the *Journal
of Education* from 1880 to 1885, was his crusade for education
in the South: "The history of the rise and progress of the American System of Common School Education . . . contains nothing
more inspiring or instructive than the plain record of what Dr.
Curry was and what he accomplished during those years from
1881 to his . . . death. "[22]

Curry's life and thoughts were in harmony with the wealthy
and influential class of white Southerners who sought to re-
build the way of life that had existed before the Civil War, to
thwart any "fanciful" ideas that might have been given blacks
during Reconstruction, and proceed to build a new Southern
community on the remnants of the Old South. Other members
of this group were men like The Reverend Amory D. Mayo and
Walter Hines Page, transplanted Southerners who had become
prominent journalists in the North. Some were politicians such
as Governor Charles Aycock of North Carolina, and others were
college presidents like Edwin A. Alderman of Tulane University
in New Orleans and Paul Barringer of the University of Virginia.
These men—the thoughtful Southerners, Jeffersonian Democrats,
Southern Progressives, or the "best white folk"—felt that they
could blend the political, social, and cultural ideals of the Old
South with the impulses and aspirations of the Industrial Revo-
lution.

Curry, himself, was not a scientific expert in pedagogy but
an educational planner, who worked out and developed a co-

herent and consistent theme for schooling that was suited to
the interests of Southern traditionalists and Northern businessmen. He became, in fact, an educational salesman with clearly
formulated postulates about the white North and South. Curry
had a perceptive understanding of Northern economic interests
in the South and what Southerners wanted for themselves. His
educational addresses focused on the material value of education, manual training, industrial training, the obligation of the
state to education, and the necessity of the South to control
the education of its black population. During the antebellum
period he had made statements that reflected a growing sensi-
tivity to both Northern and Southern interests in blacks. "African slavery is now a great fact," Curry had once said, "a political, social, industrial, humanitarian fact. Its chief product is
'King' and freights Northern vessels, drives Northern machinery, feeds Northern laborers, and clothes the entire population."
He concluded: "Northern no less than Southern capital and
labor are dependent in great degree upon it."[23] J.L.M. Curry's
views on black labor, his commitment to a North-South alliance,
and his devotion to the status quo were molded into a philosophy of education that was acceptable to most Southerners
and Northerners.[24]

Although he had been quite a prominent figure in the Old
South, the basis for Curry's educational leadership began with
the establishment of the Peabody Fund in 1867 by George
Peabody, a Massachusetts money broker who donated $1 mil-
lion that year and a second million in 1869 to aid education
in the South. Peabody was one of the first Northerners to apply
funds for this purpose. Years later, Curry was nominated by
ex-president Ulysses S. Grant as a trustee member of the Peabody Fund and was unanimously elected as second and last
general agent of the Peabody Fund on February 3, 1881.[25]
Curry's appointment was applauded by the Southern press.
The *Virginia Star*, a black newspaper, hailed J.L.M. Curry as
a "friend to the colored man."[26] The Northern foundation
undoubtedly gained added advantages by being represented
by one of the loyal sons of the Old South.

Curry's record of service to the cause of the South was outstanding. His life had afforded him the opportunity to know

most of the influential people in the South, and no one understood the feeling and interests of the white Southerner better
than he. Moreover, few Southerners understood the interests
of the North as well as Curry. He was the perfect choice to
interpret the South to the North and the North to the South.

In his vision of the new industrial South, Curry saw the
North and South as mutually dependent upon each other and
warned that the time had come for sectionalism to yield to a
new brotherhood of the Anglo-Saxon people. True reconstruction, he believed, rested not in legislative and governmental
acts but in the building of white nationalism. That Reconstruction was simply the "need of undivided Caucasian energies for
working to a wise solution the great problems which Provid-
ence has devolved upon them." According to Curry, the future
of the North was inextricably interwoven into the destiny of
the South: "The North and South are mutually dependent for
helpful offices, and for the most effective working out of their
grand destiny."[27] Let the pure Anglo-Saxon stock, Curry
urged, use its influence, money, and power to preserve the
Protestant and traditionally American culture and to control
the South's blacks.[28]

He regarded the race question as the most important issue
of his times. "Civilization certainly, Christianity probably, has
encountered no problem which surpasses in magnitude or com-
plexity, the Negro problem."[29] He viewed the education of the
black man as having far-reaching and complicated consequences
for the destiny of the white man. In an address to the legislature of Alabama, Curry said: "If the Negroes remain as co-
occupants of the land and co-citizens of the States, and we do
not lift them up, they will drag us down to industrial bank-
ruptcy, social degradation, and political corruption."[30] He was
not advocating equality for blacks. Rather, he was advising his
fellow Southerners to harness the black's economic potential
and to eliminate their political threat. "The South," Curry
maintained, "was afflicted with a devastating disease; the pres-
ence of such a multitude of Negroes, as voters and citizens,
subjects us to evils that no sagacity can avert or totally remedy."[31] One purpose of education was to cure this disease as much
as possible. Schooling was needed to counteract intemperance,

dissipation, laxity of morals, low standards of character, false views of religion. It was to instill habits of cleanliness, develop personal character, and discipline the will.[32] Curry's school was to replace the guidance of slave-masters; formal education was to replace the discipline of slavery. The failure to "train" the black would hinder the prosperity, the life, and the community of Southern whites. Curry viewed the "Negro problem" as the "white man's burden." "The docile disposition of the Afro-American . . . his facility of bad control, his irresponsibility for being the cause of conflict and peril, the drag-weight he is and must remain upon his white neighbors, enormously increase the responsibility of those who govern." In essence, the relationship between the free black and the white was to be as it was under the peculiar institution. In slavery, the relationship, the social and economic order were maintained largely through force, but in the New South, Curry pointed out, order could be maintained "not on brute force nor heavy armaments" but through education.[33]

J.L.M. Curry advocated industrial education for the black race. He differentiated manual work, which contained educational value, from trade-school teaching, by which the student gained a knowledge of some handicraft or trade. In Curry's opinion, the black who went to school specifically to learn a living was not well-educated when he left school: "It is a foolish waste of time and a deception to commit the manual training side of school work to mere mechanics, who are not educated nor trained.[34] For Curry, the real purpose of manual training was to inculcate important social and psychological values necessary to create in the blacks a recognition of their position in the New South. He knew that it was almost impossible, even if desirable, to expect the black school to keep abreast of technology. The skills that J.L.M. Curry advocated were elementary industrial skills that would aid in the process of acculturation, industrializing the pre-industrial people and organizing them to be useful in the development of the South. In short, he urged the type of education that Hampton Institute symbolized.

Curry's advocacy of education for blacks was part and parcel a result of his concern over the South's labor needs and, no less, race and nationalism. J.L.M. Curry viewed the South as a virgin land of extraordinary resources in forestry, mining, and agriculture. But its development was dependent upon labor. Ignorance and stupidity were the impediments to industrial growth. He constantly reminded his audiences that the states, cities, or localities that were the most industrious, prosperous, and progressive were those that placed emphasis on training labor.

Curry felt strongly about the need for Southern businessmen to do something about the incompetence of the South's labor force. Both the black and the white worker had made little advance over the skills and the methods of labor used in the antebellum South. It was the task of education to train and organize these masses of unskilled laborers to exploit the resources of the southland.[35]

J.L.M. Curry marshaled facts to prove education essential to the prosperity of the South. He argued that only the educated laborer could produce products that could aid America's ability to compete in the world market. Curry attributed the agricultural depression of the 1890s to the state of the labor force. He told the Populists that they were mistaken in thinking that political power could remedy the situation.

> . . . all the legislation that you could pass from now until next Christmas would not increase one iota the real returns of agriculture. There are . . . a good many fools, who are trying to find a short cut to national and individual prosperity by treating wealth as if it were a thing that could be created by statute without the intervention of labor, forgetting that the products of labor represent all that there is of wealth in a country.[36]

The relation between wealth and a productive, highly efficient labor force became the most prevalent theme in his educational propaganda.

He was convinced that capital followed the schoolhouse. Curry congratulated the South for, thus far, having freedom from strikes and from the "lawlessness of organized assertive labor."[37] The continuation of this condition, he contended, would be guaranteed through proper schooling. Curry believed that through industrial education, the Northern and Southern businessman would gain a tremendous economic return by the perpetuation of tractable labor, especially black labor. He also felt that the South could be helped by using the school to attract money from Northern industrialists. He contended that if the labor situation was made attractive enough, more Northern capital would flow southward. His ideas gained wide support in the North and a growing acceptance throughout the South. His friend and associate, Amory D. Mayo, wrote in 1881 that Curry was rallying large support to the industrial education idea. Mayo said, "It is now probably easier to persuade men of large wealth to give generously for this [industrial schooling] than for any class of educational establishments."[38]

The potential of the school to deal with the questions of material prosperity, industrialization, race, and the growth of Anglo-Saxon nationalism were not the only themes in J.L.M. Curry's educational philosophy. He argued just as sincerely that the school was to bring social, religious, and moral benefits. He had great faith in the rehabilitative powers of education. "No legislation in the United States," he said in 1883, "is more important than that which pertains to the universal education of our citizens."[39] For Curry, education had almost no limitations. The loss of territory, power, and prestige could be regained by intellectual and moral power.[40]

Neither was Curry limited in his approach to education; at least not in scope. In 1884, he made an attempt to secure national aid for education through the support of the Blair Bill. The Government Printing Office circulated copies of his remarks about the many benefits of education. He contended that education was vital to the interest of national defense. He declared that schooling could secure a better selection of rulers, that it was the best check on corruption, unwise legislation, and popular dissension. His premise was that education fostered conservative tendencies and protection of traditional American virtues, and that it was a more sensible method of social control: "General intelligence reduces the need of harsh and ex-

ternal government; makes protection of person and property
easier, surer, and more economical . . . and substitutes the
teacher for the sheriff, the workshop for the poorhouse, the
schoolhouse for prison."[41]

It is difficult, if not impossible, to measure the success of
J.L.M. Curry's educational efforts. His ideas received the warm
endorsement of his contemporaries. He was praised by John D.
Rockefeller, Andrew Carnegie, Booker T. Washington, Morris
K. Jesup, Robert Curtis Ogden, William H. Baldwin, and numerous governmental and state officials in the North and South.
In 1898, he was in Capon Springs, West Virginia, at a conference
of education in the South. Northerners and Southerners formed
this Conference on Southern Education. It brought together a
great many distinguished Northern and Southern capitalists,
educators, journalists, and clergymen. The men at the conference were, in most cases, from the wealthiest elements of society. There were also middle-class professional people in attendance; men like Arkansas's Edgar Gardner Murphy, and the North
Carolinian, Alexander J. McKelway. There were college presidents: Charles W. Dabney of Tennessee, Edwin A. Alderman
of North Carolina, Charles D. McIver of North Carolina, and
David F. Houston of Texas. They included expatriate Southerners like Walter Hines Page and George Foster Peabody and transplanted Northerners like Seaman A. Knapp.[42] At the second
meeting of the Conference on Southern Education in 1899,
the organization officially recognized the efforts of Jabez Lamar
Monroe Curry by electing him their first president. But Curry
was in the last years of his life. At the third Conference on
Southern Education, he declined reelection on account of ill
health. J.L.M. Curry died in 1903.

The man who had served under him as Vice-President of the
Conference on Southern Education, Robert Curtis Ogden, took
charge and became the new leader of the crusade for education
in the South. At the third Conference, Ogden delivered a rous-
ing paper on the need to provide the South, and particularly
the black South, with the type of education that would be economically profitable to business interests. This treatise, "The
Object of the Conference as Seen by a Northern Business Man,"

written by Ogden and delivered in precise business language, was most effective in shaping the future work of the organization. He advocated presenting the education movement to the business community as a business proposition. The time, he felt, was right for the organization to make its appeal to the "intelligent self-interest" of the practical businessman. The members were thoroughly impressed by his ideas. They unanimously elected Robert Ogden their new president, a position he would hold for thirteen years.[43]

A Northern businessman, Ogden had gained his earliest contact with the South on journeys during the 1860s, acting as agent for his New York clothing company. As a clothier he knew better than anyone the importance of Southern cotton to the North, and he understood the importance of Southern black labor to the harmonious relationship of both. He was genuinely interested in the economic contribution of black labor—a contribution he recognized as far from being exhausted. These thoughts of his had been spurred on by J.L.M. Curry and Samuel Chapman Armstrong.[44]

Armstrong had made numerous trips to the North in an effort to gain financial support for his industrial school at Hampton. Northern capitalists, however, had been slow to react, and by the time of Armstrong's death in 1893, the industrial education idea had acquired only a small group of backers. Had Samuel Chapman Armstrong lived but a few more years, he would have been able to see a massive movement for black industrial schooling. And at the head of that movement was his friend, Robert Curtis Ogden. It was soon revealed that black industrial education would be Robert Ogden's first concern as the newly elected president of the Conference on Southern Education. As Ogden later admitted, the conference was "originally interested in the South through Negro education. . . . "[45]

Ogden would succeed where Armstrong had failed. Unlike Armstrong, Ogden did not have any missionary interest in helping blacks save themselves from themselves. Industrial schooling, as he saw it, could help make a more reliable, more stable, and more efficient black labor force. If he could put his ideas into words and gain a platform, he knew that he could obtain finan-

cial backing. Samuel Chapman Armstrong had spoken the lingo
of a missionary. Ogden would speak to Northern capitalists as
a Northern capitalist.

His presidency of the Conference on Southern Education
gave him the necessary platform from which to transform his
interest in the "Negro question" into a course of action. For
the Northern and Southern business interests, J.L.M. Curry had
offered to prepare a docile labor force. The relation between
wealth, schooling, and a productive labor force had prevailed
throughout his educational propaganda. The general precept
on which Robert Curtis Ogden's philosophy of education was
postulated was similar to that of Curry. Ogden defined education and commerce as twins and industrial and educational
progress as inseparably connected.[46]

He moved swiftly to entice a larger audience of Northern
capitalists with his ideas on Southern education. From 1901
to 1913, parties of influential Northerners journeyed southward at the urging of Robert Ogden. These "Ogden Trips,"
and the luxurious train accommodations and lavish parties became a recurrent event in the solicitation of Northern monies
for Southern black and white education.[47] Ogden's biographer
wrote:

> Mr. Ogden stood for the reconciliation of North
> and South. From year to year, he brought to the
> South representative men and women of the North,
> that they might know at first hand the severe con-
> ditions with which the people of the South were
> wrestling. The result was a marked change in the
> attitude of the North toward the South and South
> toward the North. His personality was a golden clasp
> binding the two sections together.[48]

It is, indeed, clear that Ogden was interested in having the
South and North reconcile their differences. He sometimes
showed a strong sentimentality for the brotherhood of North
and South. "Dixie is the antiphon of Yankee Doodle," he ex-
claimed, "as the ends of the land come together, and harmony

of the Star-Spangled Banner is the solvent of both." He maintained that the best people in the South and North were seeing
eye-to-eye and feeling the heart throb of a common American-
ism that they had not felt since the days of early America.[49]
He reminded his Southern audiences that the Civil War was
over:

> The grass grows green and the flowers bloom these
> bright June days over the graves of the boys that
> wore the blue and the boys that wore the gray, and
> on the Memorial days, mellowed by the lapse of
> years, white-haired mothers and venerable fathers
> hark back to the days when they trembled and
> feared the battle tidings and when hearts were
> wrung by the wounds and the deaths of dear ones,
> the sacrifices to the great crisis struggle of the na-
> tion. But now the men that won sit together and
> say, 'It is better as it is'; and the losers say, 'We
> have gained more from defeat than we could have
> secured from success.'[50]

Ogden declared that the issues of the past were closed. The
thoughts of a single purpose and a common destiny were, he
contended, at last leading both the North and South to see
their problems as a whole. "The need of one state or one section is the concern of all," Ogden said. Then, turning to the
"Negro question," he asked: "Why need we be oversensitive
about our problems? In the North we have shameful questions.
. . . The questions of the South are historic and organic that
carry with them national responsibility. The case is to a degree
local, but it concerns the whole country."[51]
  By gaining Northern support for Southern black education
and Southern education in general, Ogden believed he could
aid the cause of a new nationalism. While his concern, in part,
was with helping to change the attitudes of Southerners toward Northerners, no marked change occurred in the prevailing racial attitude of most Northerners and Southerners. The
Ogden excursions had afforded a number of meetings with

North Carolina Governor, the demagogue Charles B. Aycock, and other leaders of the white supremacy movement. Aycock, elected on a platform of race supremacy and universal education, gave his endorsement to the Ogden Movement and the aims of black industrial education.[52] Upon returning from their first Southern trip, Ogden's guests indicated their compliance with the white supremacy movement.[53]

Southerners were giving careful consideration to industrial education. On occasion the discussions took on a class rather than racial perspective—for example, the consideration of adopting industrial education for both blacks and whites. William P. Trent, a self-appointed spokesman for the South and associate of Robert Curtis Ogden, saw industrial education as an aid to what he termed "Tendencies of Higher Life in the South." There was a comparative lack of social barriers in the New South—or so Trent believed—that, in fact, "renders it to a certain extent inferior to the Old; but in the near future social lines will be more strictly drawn, without doubt. . . ."[54] Education was a means to achieve that goal. His concern was with what he saw as a decaying morality and loss of the dignities and virtues of the Old South. He advocated the need to keep social and racial lines firmly implanted, thus assuring that blacks and lower-class whites would remain in their place.

One of Trent's major worries was what a little of the wrong education might do to the black. The Southern whites, Trent said, "know the Negro well, and they know that it is idle to hope that his race can be really elevated for centuries: they know also that with him it is especially true that 'a little learning is a dangerous thing.' "[55]

But he believed that degeneracy prevailed in the black race and among the lower echelon of whites and that industrial schooling could be applied to both groups. He maintained that the only value in the lower elements for the South lay in what they could do manually and technically. In his opinion, proper education for this segment of society should prepare them to serve in the general exploitation of the rich fields of Southern resources. Trent advocated that both the blacks and the lower-class whites be given industrial schooling.

> For the Negro, this sort of education [industrial education], as President Booker T. Washington has shown, will be of prime importance, but its value to the lower and middle classes of the Southern whites will be scarcely less. With all her lands and mineral treasures to be exploited, the South has paramount need of trained farmers and engineers and mechanics, and these she is now able to get from the ranks of her own sons. Then, again, the intellectual torpor of the Negroes and the poor whites will be best reached through the channels of technical and manual education.[56]

However, leading Southerners focused on the possibilities of industrial education for blacks, not whites. Southern educators devoted considerable attention and discussion to this issue. At practically every meeting of the Southern Education Association at least one paper was devoted to the topic of industrial schooling for blacks. The SEA met annually from 1899 to 1913. In 1900, George T. Winston, the white president of North Carolina College, delivered a treatise on black education at the meeting of the SEA in Richmond, Virginia. "The labor unit of the South," he contended, "is still the negro; emancipated, but ignorant, unambitious, and less trained than when a slave." Winston said, "The North and the South, government and philanthropy, education and religion, all forces, domestic, social and industrial, must combine to make the negro a better workman."[57] Winston believed that all education for blacks must be industrial, and he advocated that every program of liberal arts education for blacks be immediately abandoned:

> His colleges of law, of medicine, of theology, and of literature, science and art should be turned into schools for industrial training. Hampton Institute and Tuskegee should be duplicated in every southern state,—if possible, in each congressional district. The visionary ideals of Wendell Phillips and Frederick Douglass should give place to the practical work of

General Armstrong and Booker Washington. The
wasteful expenditure of money for negro literary
education in the public schools of the South should
be changed into profitable and useful training in industrial schools, shops and farms maintained at
public expense and under public direction, for negro education in each county or township of the
South. The entire system of public education for
the negro race, from top to bottom, should be industrial.[58]

Winston considered industrial education to be the most realistic,
most practical, and best suited program for the "uplifting" of
the South's black population. He said that he wished to "save
the negro from extinction and equip him for free existence."[59]
At the same time, he wanted to harness black labor and channel
the social and political temperament of blacks to subordination in the white South. The race issue was getting out of hand,
he believed, and he advocated a return to the past. The solution, Winston maintained, was to be found in "interest,
sympathy, and authority on the part of the whites; docility,
obedience and zeal on the part of the blacks."[60] And industrial
education would support that order of things.

Other participants in the Southern Education Association
echoed Winston's sentiments. In the final analysis, their discussions and debates usually returned to very basic fears shared by
the white South. One concern was economic, the other was
political. Paul B. Barringer, President of the University of Virginia, put the question in no uncertain terms: "We of the South
are to educate him [the black]. Shall we prepare him to be a
political antagonist? Shall we make of him an economic antagonist; or can we prevent him from becoming either, and yet
have the South as a whole improve? That is the question."
Industrial education was the answer.[61] *Harper's Magazine* had
perhaps stated the solution in even better terms twenty-six
years earlier: "Negro schools should turn out obedient, order-
ly workmen well versed in the duties of their station in life.
. . . Domestic servants should improve in honesty, possum hunt-

ing decline, and Negroes become disposed to look up to whites."[62]

Black education was not schooling for equality. Southerners were deeply concerned that somehow the education of blacks would be guided against the interests of whites. This fear largely stemmed from the fact that Northerners played such a dominant role in the industrial education movement. One Southern educator at a meeting of the Southern Education Association put the question squarely to Walter Hines Page, editor of *World's Work* and an associate of Robert Curtis Ogden. Was the real reason for Northern support of black education in the South to help blacks become equals to whites? The SEA member asked Page: "Are these two purposes, or is either of them—negro education first and negro equality—cherished by the Northern gentlemen, Mr. Ogden, for instance, who are officially prominent in the Southern Education Board?" Page's answer was brief: "Certainly not."[63]

Concurrent with white-supremacist beliefs, Robert Curtis Ogden advocated a program of education for blacks that would reenforce the old-line, class-caste order of white rule over black. After all, in his view, the Anglo-Saxon was the superior race with "the heredity of centuries of civilization while the Negro race is only a few generations removed from barbarism."[64] The near-savage blacks, therefore, could only contribute to the country by the sweat of their brow in day-to-day labor. Ogden was an advocate of the importance of black labor to the economic stability of the South (and the economic importance of the South to the whole of America). "The prosperity of the South," he said, "largely depends upon the productive power of the black man."[65] Industrial education would provide the "proper" training necessary for the greater exploitation of that labor minus, however, any notions of racial equality and the rights of full citizenship.

His years in the New York clothing industry and as an associate of the Wanamaker enterprises of Philadelphia afforded Robert Curtis Ogden numerous connections that he called upon for support of the Southern education movement and development of the Southern Education Board. He knew the fathers, sons, and grandsons of the Northern elite. His partnership with the father of Morris K. Jesup illustrates this connection. The young Jesup, in addition to distinction as a leading Northern magnate in Southern railroads, became an influential member of the Southern Education Board. The prominent George F. Gates, father of Frederick T. Gates, was an old Ogden associate. Frederick T. Gates, a Baptist clergyman and New York business executive, became one of the first directors of the Southern Education Board.

In addition to coopting men of wealth, Ogden also realized the tremendous necessity of having at least a segment of the press on his side.[66] He was certain to have the press on his side when he ventured southward. Pleased with Lyman Abbott's *Outlook*, he gave Abbott a permanent place of respect as a charter member in the industrial education crusade. Abbott later served on the Southern Education Board. The *Outlook* always commented favorably on the Southern education movement.

The Southern Education Board, which Ogden founded in 1901, devoted its energies "entirely to a propaganda for education" in the South,[67] inviting Northern monies for Southern education and attempting to console the many Southerners suspicious of the North. Jabez Lamar Monroe Curry pointed out that at its first meeting the Southern Education Board moved to establish a harmonious relationship with the Slater and Peabody funds for black education.[68] The *Nation* predicted that the board would be of benefit to everyone.[69]

The SEB, however, was interested in the education of blacks and in the welfare of whites. Ogden saw no paradox in this philosophy. He could openly state to Archer M. Huntington, "The efforts of our Southern Education Board are directed to the educational welfare of all the people, and, as a matter of fact, are more deeply concerned with white than black."[70]

The independence of the Southern Education Board lasted one year. In 1902, Ogden and associates unofficially incorporated with a newly established body, the Rockefeller-sponsored General Education Board. Typical of Rockefeller, once he made up his mind on the value and soundness of an undertaking, he moved to control it. Rockefeller would make sure that the industrial education crusade received the financial backing it needed. Thus, as Ogden explained to Andrew Carnegie in 1904, the General Education Board was "organized to receive and disburse money."[71]

Why was the board formed? The story of Rockefeller and his various business escapades has seemingly been summed up elsewhere.[72] Significantly, no student of the history of Standard Oil or the life of John D. Rockefeller has been able to determine every business enterprise in which Rockefeller had a hand. His connection with Southern cottonseed oil is one of the many unwritten chapters of Rockefeller history. It is understandable that Rockefeller was very concerned with the Southern scene. It was quite in keeping with the efforts by big business in the late nineteenth and early twentieth centuries to expand and monopolize and tinge it all with corporate liberalism,[73] that Northern magnates like Rockefeller attempted to stabilize the South. Indeed, the railroads of the South and North were merged. And clearly Northern capital was invested in the South. Henry H. Rogers and J. H. Flagler were two Rockefeller associates who headed large industries in the South. Rogers, President of Standard Oil in the South, was a paramount figure in Southern railroads. Flagler's role in the story of cottonseed oil has been discussed earlier. To all concerned the establishment and securing of a well-trained, stable, and docile Southern labor force would be a great benefit. It was out of that desire and the hope of influencing public sentiment that the Rockefeller General Education Board was founded.

The initial officers and members as listed in *The General Education Board: An Account of its Activities, 1902-1914,* were as follows:

OFFICERS

CHAIRMAN	William H. Baldwin	*1902-1904*
	Robert C. Ogden	*1905-1906*
	Frederick T. Gates	*1907-*
SECRETARY	Wallace Buttrick	*1902-*

ASSISTANT	William H. Heck	*1903-1905*
SECRETARIES	Ebden Charles Gage	*1905-*
	Abraham Flexner	*1913-*
TREASURER	George Foster Peabody	*1902-1909*
	Louis G. Myers	*1910-*
ASSISTANT TREASURER	L. M. Dashell	*1914-*

MEMBERS

William H. Baldwin	*1902-1905*
Jabez L. M. Curry	*1902-1903*
Frederick T. Gates	*1902-*
Daniel C. Gilman	*1902-1908*
Morris K. Jesup	*1902-1908*
Robert C. Ogden	*1902-1913*
Walter H. Page	*1902-*
George Foster Peabody	*1902-1912*
John D. Rockefeller, Jr.	*1902-*
Albert Shaw	*1902-*
Wallace Buttrick	*1902-*
Starr J. Murphy	*1904-*
William R. Harper	*1905-1906*
Hugh H. Hanna	*1905-1912*
E. Benjamin Andrews	*1905-1912*
Edwin A. Alderman	*1906-*
Hollis B. Frissell	*1906-*
Harry Pratt Judson	*1906-*
Charles W. Eliot	*1908-*
Andrew Carnegie	*1908-*
Edgar L. Marston	*1909-*
Wickliffe Rose	*1910-*
Jerome D. Greene	*1912-*
Anson Phelps Stokes	*1912-*
Abraham Flexner	*1914-*
George E. Vincent	*1914-*

The board was a well-chosen group of Northern capitalists, educators, and other proponents of industrial schooling. Noticeably, the board also included clergymen. This is not surprising for in them Rockefeller saw a general adherence to the ideals of conservatism and economic stability.[74]

Frederick T. Gates of the General Education Board was a Baptist clergyman and business executive. Gates made an early friendship with John D. Rockefeller and became the "guiding force" in many of Rockefeller's enterprises. It was Gates who advised Rockefeller about philanthropies and foundations: "These funds should be so large that to become a trustee of one of them would be to make a man at once a public character. They should be so large that their administration would be as much a matter of public concern, inquiry and public criticism as any of the functions of the Government are now."[75] Rockefeller followed Gates's advice closely. The General Education Board launched the careers of many important governmental officials.[76]

The general attitude of the board toward blacks was articulated by the GEB's first president, William H. Baldwin. Baldwin had become interested in the "Negro question" during his years with the Southern Railway. He considered blacks to be immensely valuable and properly suited for work in the South. Baldwin wanted to direct them and harness their full economic potential. According to him, this could be achieved through proper education. But, at the same time, he warned, "Negroes must not be educated out of their natural environment."[77] Industrial schooling was the answer:

> The potential economic value of the Negro population properly educated is infinite and incalculable. In the Negro is the opportunity of the South. Time has proven that he is best fitted to perform the heavy labor in the Southern states. The negro and the mule is the only combination so far to grow cotton. The South needs him; but the South needs him educated to be a suitable citizen. Properly directed he is the best possible laborer to meet the climactic conditions of the South. He will willingly fill the more menial positions, and do the heavy

work, at less wages, than the American white man
or any foreign race which has yet come to our shores.
This will permit the Southern white laborer to perform the more expert labor, and to leave the fields,
the mines, and the simpler trades for the Negro.[78]

Baldwin's views were publicly praised by Andrew Carnegie,
Hollis B. Frissell, and Charles W. Eliot.[79] They were also clearly
endorsed by Frederick T. Gates and Wallace Buttrick.[80]

The board's philosophy was exemplified in the thinking and
actions of Booker T. Washington. Washington assured Northern
capitalists and their Southern counterparts that industrial education promised a reliable and cheap labor supply and that racial friction, which was becoming the order of the day, would
diminish. In *Up From Slavery* (1901), Washington professed
his adherence to the new industrial order. In a speech before
the Southern Industrial Convention, he voiced his acceptance
of the New South. He stated that the black man was a friend
of the South and had proven this by being "almost a stranger
to strikes, lockouts, and labor wars." Washington's views on
labor and race were the reason for his acceptance by industrialists. His views so impressed Andrew Carnegie that he bestowed
on Washington enough money to guarantee him and his wife an
income for life.[81]

The contribution of Booker Washington to securing the black
labor force for exploitation was significant. He contributed to
the division between Southern black and white laborers. In the
large Birmingham district of the Tennessee Coal, Iron and Railroad Company, Washington came forth in support of nonco-
operation between the district's black and white workers.[82]
H. H. Rogers used Washington to placate labor. He added a
special car to his Virginia Railway on which Booker Washington
was to ride and give talks to black workers. In the summer of
1909, Washington made a tour on the Virginia Railway from
Norfolk, Virginia, to Deepwater, West Virginia, making over
forty speeches on behalf of industrial education and "economic
development."[83]

It is little wonder that Northern industrialists with economic
interests in the South viewed Washington favorably. J. P. Morgan

and H. H. Rogers expressed their fondness of Booker Washington. Andrew Carnegie liked him, as did John D. Rockefeller, Robert Curtis Ogden, Julius Rosenwald of Sears, Roebuck and Company, and Collis P. Huntington.[84] Not well known is the fact that Huntington gave thousands of dollars to Tuskegee.[85] The industrialist dearest to Washington, however, was William H. Baldwin. After the death of Samuel Chapman Armstrong, Baldwin became Washington's new mentor, his closest white adviser. In a sense, Baldwin took General Armstrong's place.[86]

Understandably, then, Booker T. Washington and Tuskegee Institute (and Hampton Institute) received the full backing of the General Education Board, but not without strings attached. Tuskegee's finances were controlled and carefully monitored by the GEB.[87] The board had the school's educational program under careful surveillance. This was unnecessary, however, for Tuskegee and its Founder's devotion to the industrial education idea was total, as Paul Monroe usually reported to the board in his many surveys of the school. On one occasion, Monroe had observed an English class in session and wrote to the GEB about the successful lesson he had witnessed that day:

> In a class in English composition two boys, among others, had placed their written work upon the board, one having written upon "Honor" in the most stilted language, with various historical references which meant nothing to himself or to his class mates—the whole paragraph evidently being drawn from some outside source. The other wrote upon "My Trade"— Blacksmithing—and told in a simple and direct way his day's work, the nature of the general course of training, and the use he expected to make of his training when completed.[88]

Booker Washington kept the board informed of his efforts to carry out the industrial education idea. After his speech on June 18, 1906, in Montgomery, Alabama, on the need for less labor agitation, Washington sent a copy of the speech to Wallace Buttrick and a letter in which he explained how he had spoken "successfully" on the labor question.[89]

He gave the board detailed reports on Tuskegee's accomplishments. In 1907, he told the Board:

> Those upon the grounds constantly keep before them the fact that the school must each year send out leaders who will teach the Negro people the dignity of labor. . . . With few exceptions Tuskegee graduates are the leaders among the colored people of their communities. Not only is this true, but in nearly every one of the Southern States men and women from Tuskegee Institute have founded institutions, or appear as Principals in institutions that are so large and strong that they are reproducing the work of the parent school; they, too, are sending out leaders. The demand for these men and women is just as great or greater from white citizens who wish their services utilized in connection with many of the industrial enterprises of the South.[90]

Nevertheless, the board found fault with Tuskegee. Recurring incidents of student unrest at the school upset them. It was reported to Robert Curtis Ogden that "perfect discipline . . . as seen in all phases of the work at Hampton are not as evident at Tuskegee."[91] Washington attempted to explain to the board the 1903 student strike at the school, when students had rebelled against the institute's policies and practices. He submitted a letter to William H. Baldwin in which he gave his interpretation of why the strike had occurred.[92] Baldwin was obviously not impressed. He reprimanded Washington for not having handled the situation better.[93]

But Booker T. Washington was their man. His efforts at keeping black and white laborers separated, his adherence to education for subserviency combined with his increasing prominence made him an important asset to the New South movement. The crusaders for industrial education were so thoroughly impressed by the suitability of Booker Washington that they embraced him as the great Black Moses of the South.[94] As Merle Curti stated, "Insofar as Washington defended the status quo, he was their man, and the industrial barons raised him to great heights."[95]

Tuskegee Institute was very much a Northern entity. Unlike Hampton with its all-white staff, Tuskegee with its all-black staff and prominent black leader did not receive substantial financial support from the white South. Washington was forced to seek funds for his school in the North. Consequently, Tuskegee owed its continued existence to Northern industrialists. This served only to heighten Southern dislike for the school. "The feeling appears to be born," Washington was advised, "of the impression that the Institute is doing little or nothing for Alabama, and of the fact that the Institute is supported and managed by people at a distance."[96]

The crusaders for industrial education did not confine their interests to the South. They considered developing schools similar to Hampton and Tuskegee in the North. They believed that the movement had within itself the "possibilities of the highest usefulness."[97] The corollary to this may well have been the increasing need for black labor at the menial level in Northern industry. Also, since blacks were considered to be best suited for domestic service and similar positions of mediocrity, they were sought for such work in the more wealthy areas of the North. Robert Curtis Ogden postulated that there existed a vast field for domestic employment in New York: "The English, Irish, French and Swiss are holding places in domestic service in this city [New York] that would naturally belong to the colored people. . . . "[98]

Many Southerners and Northerners questioned the motives and objectives of the crusade for black industrial education. One Southern citizen, contemplating the movement and its effect on the Southern labor market, wrote to Robert Ogden that black education would increase the competition between white and black workers.[99] There were those who charged the General Education Board with making donations to black schools instead of white.[100] In addition to W.E.B. Du Bois, many blacks were critical of the educational crusaders and their aim of industrial schooling for Southern blacks. Dissenting opinion on industrial education was emphasized by the growth in unpopularity of Booker T. Washington.[101]

The GEB received reports attesting to the dislike for Washington in many sections of the country. Edgar Gardner Murphy said, "Mr. Washington was never so intensely unpopular." Murphy pointed to the "showiness" of "so large an institution as Tuskegee" and the "power" and "prestige" in the command of Booker Washington as cause for much of the hostility against him.[102] "How can the Negro go against Booker T. Washington?" wrote Margaret Deland to Robert Ogden. "Mr. Washington is the one voice crying in the wilderness, I am very sure; but his foes are of his own household!" Referring to the hostilities against Washington as demonstrated by the "Boston Riot," Deland asserted: "That dreadful outbreak . . . and the antagonism of such men as [W.E.B.] Du Bois, make the outlook profoundly discouraging. . . ."[103]

Black and whites questioned the program of Northern-controlled education for the South. Many were particularly concerned with the power of the General Education Board, which was founded and dominated by Northerners. Oswald Garrison Villard commented on how many blacks thoroughly distrusted the Board. Villard, a supporter of industrial education, told of the desire by blacks and himself to see blacks represented on the General Education Board. The GEB, however, had no intention of letting possible antagonists become members. Ogden answered:

> There is no logical demand for representation in
> either Board from any person except the donors.
> I find, upon contact with the colored people, that
> an utterly erroneous notion concerning the func-
> tions of the General Education Board prevails.
> Very many suppose that it asserts a general control
> over education in the South and that it also assumes
> to direct the channels of philanthropy for Negro
> education. Nothing could be further removed from
> the actual facts. I think that this misunderstanding
> is the basis of the demand from the colored people
> for representation in the Board.[104]

If circumstances somehow necessitated the GEB to place a black face on the board, there was no question as to who that appointee would be. "Personally," Robert Curtis Ogden, the new chairman of the board, concluded in his reply to Villard, "I should be delighted to welcome [Booker T.] Washington in the General Education Board. . . . I have carefully reviewed the colored men personally known to me and I can see none other than Washington that would be fitted for the place."[105]

Criticism of the board was well justified. As the dispenser of most major funds for black education in the South, the GEB was an educational power broker.[106] W.E.B. Du Bois understood this:

> When later there came an attempt on the part of the
> Southern Education Board, and afterwards of the
> General Education Board, to form a working pro-
> gram . . . it gradually became an understood principle
> of action that colored teachers would be encouraged
> in colored schools; that the races in the schools
> should be separated socially; that colored schools
> should be chiefly industrial; and that every effort
> should be made to conciliate Southern white public
> opinion. Schools which were successfully carrying
> out this program could look for further help from
> organized philanthropy. Other schools . . . could not.[107]

By channeling "philanthropic" support to those institutions and individuals who supported the industrial education idea, the GEB assured that industrial schooling would be the dominant type of education in the black South.

Industrial education meant immediate financial gain for the educational crusaders. The Southern Improvement Company is a prime example. An organization for the economic penetration of the South by Northern investors, the S.I.C.'s properties included Southern farms, cotton plantations, cotton mills, and cottonseed oil mills, all of which were run on cheap black labor. Robert Ogden openly admitted that the dominant labor force utilized on S.I.C. enterprises was black, and he attempted to explain how the company's use of that labor was for the blacks' own benefit. The S.I.C.'s "major objective in regards to the Negro," he declared at a meeting with Southern businessmen, "is with the building of character through business."[108]

Ogden, the major stockholder in the S.I.C., reported to the company's other stockholders in New York that profits were increasing.[109] He conducted S.I.C. affairs from the headquarters of the General Education Board, 54 William Street, New York, New York. There could be no doubt of the link between the Southern Improvement Company and the educational crusade. By mid-1905, the S.I.C. officially changed its name to the Southern Improvement Company and Southern Education Society.

Through the S.I.C., Robert Curtis Ogden cultivated a business alliance with his son-in-law, treasurer of Hampton Institute and stockholder in the S.I.C., Alexander Purves. Purves and Ogden collaborated on many business deals. In 1901, the correspondence between the two men indicated they were most desirous of obtaining land near Tuskegee, where a black labor force was at their disposal.[110]

Ogden and the other educational crusaders gained a reputation for desiring quick profits. When Purves died, Robert Ogden was solicited by Purves's associate for many years, Andrew Paine. Paine wanted assistance in contacting Northern capitalists. From his loan office in Tuskegee, Alabama, Paine wrote Ogden:

> At the time of Purves' death, he was about to put me in correspondence with capitalists in Philadelphia for the purpose of making loans on farm lands in this state, and had he lived I have no doubt that such arrangements could have been made. Now knowing that you have an extensive acquaintance with Northern capitalists, I write to try to enlist you in my plan. . . . I loan money strictly on farm lands on a basis of 50% of the value and consider this the finest security in the world. Now I know that you are a very busy man, but thought perhaps that you would not be

> adverse to adding to your income without any trouble to yourself. If you could place loans for me I would be willing to allow you a royalty of say 1% on all loans made by me.[111]

After further correspondence, and the record is not clear as to the final terms of their agreement, Ogden consented.

In 1906, William H. Scoville, an S.I.C. finance employee, reported to Ogden at his New York office that blacks on the company's plantations "commenced picking cotton August 25th, and I presume will be able to store considerable. . . . "[112] The S.I.C. owned a number of prosperous farms on which profit was made by tenant tenure. With cheap black labor readily available, investment returns continuously increased.[113]

The correspondence between Robert Curtis Ogden and the Bookerite Robert R. Moton attests to the economic interests of the industrial education crusaders under the banner of black improvement. This correspondence depicts their version of philanthropy for the black South. Moton, writing to Ogden, said that he thought "this scheme [the S.I.C.] . . . opens up a large opportunity for Northern men of means to invest money in this sort of thing and get a reasonable interest on their investment and at the same time help the Negro. . . . " In reference to the death of Alexander Purves, Moton added: "He [Purves] would have, without question, shown that it was possible to combine business and philanthropy and make them work out to the success of both."[114] The interests of the industrial education crusaders, however, was not to be confined within the geographical boundaries of the South or of the nation.

NOTES

1. Booker T. Washington, "The Awakening of the Negro," *Atlantic Monthly* 78 (1896), pp. 327-328.

2. Clara Mildred Thompson, *Reconstruction in Georgia, Economic, Social, Political* (New York: Columbia Univ. Press, 1915), pp. 311, 315.

3. *Commercial and Financial Chronicle* 5 (23 November 1867), p.

643; 9 (3 July 1869), p. 3; 10 (4 June 1870), p. 722. The *Chronicle* is a business weekly started in New York in 1866. The press of the day offered complimentary remarks about it. It is a traditionally reliable source of business news.

4. "Baldwin, William Henry," *Dictionary of American Biography*, ed. Dumas Malone (New York: Scribner's, 1928); Southern Railway Company, "Annual Meeting of Stockholders," *Proceedings* (Richmond, Va.: 1900-1920).

5. The Virginia Railway Company, *First Annual Report for the Fiscal Year Ending June 30, 1910*; Booker T. Washington, *My Larger Education* (New York: Doubleday, Page & Co., 1911), pp. 72-73.

6. C. Vann Woodward, *Origins of the New South, 1877-1913* (Baton Rouge, La.: Louisiana State University Press, 1970), p. 126.

7. Ethel Armes, *The Story of Coal and Iron in Alabama* (Birmingham, Ala.: Published under the auspices of the Chamber of Commerce, University Press, Cambridge, Mass., 1910); Ida M. Tarbell, *The Life of Elbert H. Gary* (New York: Appleton, 1925), pp. 196-201.

8. *Chronicle* 1 (23 September 1865), p. 387.

9. Ibid. (11 November 1865), p. 612.

10. Ibid. (20 January 1866), p. 68.

11. Ibid. (20 June 1868), p. 262.

12. Ibid. (11 September 1886), p. 302.

13. John Graham Brooks, *An American Citizen: The Life of William H. Baldwin* (New York: Houghton Mifflin, 1910), p. 171.

14. *Report of United States Industrial Commission* 7 (1900), pp. 59-60.

15. *Southern Workman*, October 1900, p. 397.

16. Lorenzo Greene and Carter G. Woodson, *The Negro Wage Earner* (Washington, D. C.: Van Rees, 1930), p. 130.

17. *Birmingham Daily News*, 20 April 1894.

18. U.S. Census, *Ninth-Twelfth Census, 1870-1900: Population*; Herbert Gutman, "Black Workers and Labor Unions in Birmingham, Alabama," Unpublished Manuscript, 1971, p. 4.

19. U.S. Senate Committee on Education and Labor, *Testimony Before the Committee to Investigate the Relations Between Capital and Labor* 4 (Washington, D. C., 1885), pp. 47, 483.

20. Greene and Woodson, p. 154. The Texas cotton oil syndicate was a leading force in the American Cottonseed Oil Trust.

21. W.E.B. Du Bois, *Autobiography* (New York: International Pubs., 1969), p. 229.

22. Amory D. Mayo, "Services of Doctor Curry in Connection with the Peabody Fund," *Report of the Commission of Education for the Year 1903* 1 (Washington, D.C., 1905), pp. 524-525.

23. Edwin A. Alderman and Armistead C. Gordon, *J.L.M. Curry: A Biog-*

raphy (New York: The Macmillan Company, 1911), p. 138.

24. Ibid.

25. *Proceedings of the Trustees of the Peabody Fund* 2 (Cambridge, Mass., 1875-1916), p. 368.

26. Quoted in W. J. Lewis, *The Educational Speaking of J.L.M. Curry* (Ann Arbor, Mich.: Univ. Microfilms, Ph.D. Dissertation, 1955), p. 63.

27. J.L.M. Curry, *The Southern States of the American Union* (New York: G. P. Putnam, 1894), pp. 267, 245.

28. Lewis, p. 103.

29. J.L.M. Curry, "Difficulties, Complications, and Limitations Connected with the Education of the Negro," *Report of Commissioner of Education for the Year 1894-1895* 2 (Washington, D.C., 1896), p. 1367.

30. *Proceedings of the Trustees of the Peabody Fund* 3, p. 61.

31. Lewis, p. 252.

32. *Proceedings of the Trustees of the Peabody Fund* 3, p. 61.

33. *Proceedings of the Trustees of the John F. Slater Fund* (Baltimore, Md., 1899), p. 14.

34. Ibid., p. 10.

35. Lewis, p. 113.

36. Ibid., pp. 112-113.

37. Merle Curti, *The Social Ideas of American Educators* (New York: Scribner's, 1935), p. 277.

38. Mayo, p. 11.

39. J.L.M. Curry, "National Aid to Education," *Circulars of Information of the Bureau of Education* 3 (Washington, D.C., 1884), p. 261.

40. Ibid., p. 262.

41. Ibid.

42. Woodward, pp. 396-397.

43. Charles William Dabney, *Universal Education in the South* (New York: Arno Press, [1936] 1969), p. 12.

44. General Armstrong to Robert Curtis Ogden, 25 January 1879, *Robert Curtis Ogden Papers*, Library of Congress; Robert Curtis Ogden to General Samuel Chapman Armstrong, 20 September 1884, *Ogden Papers*; Robert Curtis Ogden to General Samuel Chapman Armstrong, 14 February 1885 and 19 February 1885, *Ogden Papers*; Robert Curtis Ogden, *Samuel Chapman Armstrong: A Sketch* (New York: Fleming H. Revell Company, 1894), pp. 22-25 and passim.

45. *Proceedings of the Fourth Conference for Education in the South* (Winston-Salem, N.C., 1901), p. 6.

46. Robert Curtis Ogden, "Popular Education: The Power of Industrial Progress," undated speech at a gathering of the leaders of Southern manufacturing, p. 5, *Ogden Papers*.

47. The *Ogden Papers* reveal a steady stream of correspondence from

Ogden to Wall Street, and everyone who was "anyone" was invited to journey with Ogden southward. For accounts of the "Ogden Trips," see Samuel C. Mitchell, *Robert Curtis Ogden: A Leader in the Educational Renaissance of the South* (Unpublished Biography, *Ogden Papers*, undated); Edward Ingle, *The Ogden Movement: An Educational Monopoly in the Making* (Baltimore: Manufacturer's Record Pub. Co., 1908); Louis R. Harlan, *Separate and Unequal* (New York: Atheneum, 1968), pp. 75-83; C. Vann Woodward, *Origins of the New South;* Henry Allen Bullock, *A History of Negro Education in the South: From 1619 to the Present* (New York: Praeger, 1970).

48. Mitchell, p. 2.

49. Ogden, "Popular Education: The Power of Industrial Progress," p. 5.

50. Ibid.

51. Ibid.

52. Dabney, pp. 280-281; R.D.W. Connor and Clarence Poe, *The Life and Speeches of Charles Brantley Aycock* (New York: Doubleday, Page and Company, 1912), pp. 410-419; Edwin A. Alderman, "Charles Brantley Aycock: An Appreciation," *North Carolina Historical Review* 1 (July 1924).

53. Harlan, *Separate and Unequal,* p. 80.

54. William P. Trent, "Tendencies of Higher Life in the South," *Atlantic Monthly* 79 (1897), p. 775.

55. Ibid., p. 772.

56. Ibid., p. 773.

57. *Proceedings of the Southern Education Association* (Richmond, Va., December 1900), p. 116.

58. Ibid.

59. Ibid., p. 117.

60. Ibid.

61. Ibid., p. 128.

62. *Harper's* 49 (1874), p. 462.

63. Southern Education Board, "Southern Education," Knoxville, Tenn. Publishers, Vol. 1, Nos. 8 and 9, May 7, 1903.

64. Ogden, "Popular Education: The Power of Industrial Progress," p. 3.

65. Robert Curtis Ogden, "Concerning the Negro," undated, *Ogden Papers.*

66. Criticism from the *Post* damaged the Wanamaker Company in the late 1800s. Ogden was an associate with that company. "The Evening Post, it degrades journalism," wrote Ogden. Furthermore, he added, "The editor of the Evening Post is an Irish ass." [Robert Curtis Ogden to Curry, 21 June 1890, *Ogden Papers.*]

67. Robert Curtis Ogden to Andrew Carnegie, 30 January 1904, *Andrew Carnegie Papers*, Library of Congress.

68. J.L.M. Curry to Daniel C. Gilman, 30 August 1901, *Curry Papers*, Library of Congress.

69. *Nation* 74 (13 March 1902), p. 202.

70. Robert Curtis Ogden to Archer M. Huntington, 27 February 1904, *Ogden Papers*.

71. Robert Curtis Ogden to Andrew Carnegie, 30 January 1904, *Carnegie Papers*. Also see note 106.

72. See Ida M. Tarbell, *The History of the Standard Oil Company* (New York: MacMillian, 1904).

73. For a discussion, see Gabriel Kolko, *The Triumph of Conservatism* (Chicago: Quadrangle, 1963), and James Weinstein, *The Corporate Ideal in the Liberal State* (Boston: Beacon Press, 1967).

74. See Clyde Ferguson, "The Political and Social Ideas of John D. Rockefeller and Andrew Carnegie" (Ph.D. Dissertation, University of Illinois, 1951).

75. Jules Abels, *The Rockefeller Billions* (New York: MacMillian, 1965), pp. 327-328.

76. For example, John Foster Dulles was chairman of the General Education Board from 1950 to 1952. Dean Rusk served as president of the Board from 1952 to 1961.

77. William H. Baldwin, "The Present Problem of Negro Education," *Journal of Social Science* 37 (1899). This was an address read on Tuesday, 5 September 1899.

78. Ibid., p. 58.

79. "Discussion of the Work of the Hampton Institute and the Bearing of Industrial Education on Race Problems in the South," *Proceedings of the Meeting of the Armstrong Association*, February 12, 1904.

80. Robert H. Bremner, *American Philanthropy* (Chicago: University of Chicago Press, 1960), pp. 111-112.

81. Emma L. Thornbrough, ed., *Booker T. Washington* (N.J.: Prentice-Hall, 1969), pp. 7-8.

82. *Birmingham Age-Herald*, 1 April 1899; Horace Mann Bond, *Negro Education in Alabama: A Study in Cotton and Steel* (New York: Associated Publishers, 1939), pp. 168-170.

83. Washington, *My Larger Education*, p. 72; *Southern Letter* 25, No. 12 (December 1909), p. 3.

84. Thornbrough, p. 8.

85. There are approximately three hundred letters in the Huntington

papers on contributions to Tuskegee and Hampton. See, for example: Booker T. Washington to Collis P. Huntington, 20 December 1890 and 15 August 1891; Samuel Chapman Armstrong to Collis P. Huntington, 4 January 1878 and 16 September 1882; and miscellaneous financial statements, building plans, and deeds, *Collis P. Huntington Papers*, Syracuse University.

86. Louis R. Harlan, *Booker T. Washington: The Making of a Black Leader, 1856-1901* (New York: Oxford University Press, 1972), p. 216.

87. For example, see the reports of Daniel C. Smith, Certified Public Accountant of New York, to Robert Curtis Ogden, 31 May 1906 and 3 June 1906; Wallace Buttrick to Booker T. Washington, 11 July 1906, *General Education Board Papers*, File No. Ala. 12, Series 1, Rockefeller Archives. The GEB was impressed by Hampton and its emphasis on "learning to work rather than on book learning." [Wallace Buttrick to Carnegie, 14 February 1905, *General Education Board Papers*, File No. Ala. 12, Series 1.] See also H. B. Frissell, Principal of Hampton Institute, to Buttrick, 16 February 1907; and "Report on Training at Hampton Institute, to General Education Board, February 4, 1905," *General Education Board Papers*, File No. Va. 38, Series 1.

88. Paul Monroe to Wallace Buttrick, 6 May 1904, p. 2, *General Education Board Papers*, File No. Ala. 12, Series 1.

89. Booker T. Washington to Wallace Buttrick, 18 June 1906, *General Education Board Papers*, File No. Ala. 12, Series 1.

90. "Confidential Report of the Principal of the Tuskegee Normal and Industrial Institute to the Trustees, For Year Ending May 31, 1907," p. 1, *General Education Board Papers*, File No. Ala. 12, Series 1.

91. Lawrence Dutton to Robert Curtis Ogden, 16 April 1906, *General Education Board Papers*, File No. Ala. 12, Series 1.

92. Booker T. Washington to William H. Baldwin, 23 October 1903, *General Education Board Papers*, File No. Ala. 12, Series 1.

93. William H. Baldwin to Booker T. Washington, 27 October 1903, *General Education Board Papers*, File No. Ala. 12, Series 1.

94. H. L. Wayland to Robert Curtis Ogden, 9 October 1896, *Ogden Papers*.

95. Curti, p. 299.

96. Seth Low to Booker T. Washington, 12 December 1906, *Booker T. Washington Papers*, Library of Congress.

97. Robert Curtis Ogden to Rev. Frissell, 7 March 1900, *Ogden Papers*.

98. Robert Curtis Ogden to Mrs. Gilman, 21 May 1903, *Ogden Papers*.

99. Rev. Samuel M. Smith to Robert Curtis Ogden, 27 March 1905, *Ogden Papers*. For further insight on the Southern criticism, see Edward Ingle, *The Ogden Movement: An Educational Monopoly in the Making*.

100. Clippings from the old *Baltimore Journal* (April 1905) in *Ogden Papers*.

101. What soon became known as the "Boston Riot" was a clash during the evening of 30 July 1903 between protesters and sympathizers of industrial education and the leadership of Booker T. Washington. Monroe Trotter, founder and editor of the *Boston Guardian* and outspoken black anti-Bookerite, led a protest that evening just as Booker Washington prepared to take the speaker's platform at a gathering of black Bostonians. Simultaneously, fist fights broke out throwing the meeting into total chaos. As a result, a number of blacks were arrested, among them Monroe Trotter. The *New York Times* called the riot "a most disgraceful and lamentable episode," perpetrated by individuals who were "all for war and for a rush into full equality of every kind, deserved or undeserved." [*New York Times*, 1 August 1903, p. 6.] Monroe Trotter pinpointed black discontent with Washington in a question he prepared but never got a chance to ask at the Boston gathering. Trotter wrote, "Don't you know you would help the race more by exposing the new form of slavery just outside the gates of Tuskegee than by preaching submission?" [Quoted in Stephen R. Fox, *The Guardian of Boston* (New York: Antheneum, 1971), p. 50.]

102. Edgar Gardner Murphy to Robert Curtis Ogden, 8 March 1904, *Ogden Papers*.

103. Margaret Deland to Robert Curtis Ogden, 29 April 1904, *Ogden Papers*.

104. Robert Curtis Ogden to Oswald Garrison Villard, 11 March 1905, *Ogden Papers*.

105. Ibid.

106. The Southern Education Board received its financial support via the General Education Board. It was not until 1914 that the S.E.B. officially made the leadership of the G.E.B. known by formally dissolving and incorporating into the General Education Board. [*The General Education Board: An Account of Its Activities, 1902-1914*, especially pages 8, 154-160.] "Parallel to the Southern Education Board there has been formed the Board of the General Education Fund for the disbursement of money for educational purposes." (Opening Address) [*Fifth Annual Conference for Education in the South*, Athens, Georgia, 24 April 1902.] "Besides this interlocking directorate," stated Hollis B. Frissell, "the Peabody and Slater Boards are now acting very largely through the General Education Board." [Hollis B. Frissell to Archer M. Huntington, 17 February 1903, *Hollis B. Frissell Papers*, Hampton Institute.] Also see Donald Spivey, "The Role of Industrial Education for the Black South, 1866-1915" (M.A. Thesis, University of Illinois, 1972), p. 96, and "White

Philanthropy and Black Education" (Undergraduate Honors Thesis, University of Illinois, 1971), pp. 38, 54.

107. W.E.B. Du Bois, *Autobiography*, p. 233.

108. Ogden delivered this speech at a small meeting of Southern businessmen late in 1901. Notes on the speech, dated 1901, are in the *Ogden Papers*. For additional reflections on Ogden's idea of the work ethic, see *"Business Idealism"* (June 1905), found in *Ogden Papers*.

109. Robert Curtis Ogden to Stockholders of the Southern Improvement Company, 2 May 1902 and 7 November 1905, Alexander Purves to Emmet Scott, 3 May 1901, *Ogden Papers;* "Report of William H. Scoville to Robert Curtis Ogden, 1908," *General Education Board Papers*, Box 203; "Report of Harris Barrett to Robert C. Ogden, January 18, 1910," *General Education Board Papers*, Box 203.

110. Alexander Purves to Robert Curtis Ogden, 7 January 1901, *Ogden Papers*.

111. Andrew Paine to Robert Curtis Ogden, 4 June 1905, *Ogden Papers*.

112. William H. Scoville to Robert Curtis Ogden, 18 September 1906, *Ogden Papers*.

113. Robert Curtis Ogden to S.I.C. Stockholders, 7 November 1905, *Ogden Papers*. Harris Barrett, reporting to Ogden from the South, told of increased profits from S.I.C. tenant farms. [Harris Barrett to Robert Curtis Ogden, 18 January 1910, *Ogden Papers*.] The S.I.C. was apparently linked to the Rockefeller camp. See Edward Chase Kirkland, *Industry Comes of Age* (Chicago: Quadrangle, 1961), p. 84.

114. Robert R. Moton to Robert Curtis Ogden, 24 October 1908, *Ogden Papers*.

5

THE PAN-AFRICAN IMPACT OF BLACK INDUSTRIAL SCHOOLING

Toward a Conclusion

> In the presence of such ominous conditions and
> dangerous trends, what is the way of escape from
> the impending peril to our civilization? My emphat-
> ic answer is that the way of Booker T. Washington
> is clearly the way out of our present threatening
> dilemma.
>
> —Thomas Jesse Jones (1919)

Industrial education was extended beyond the "Negro problem"
in the United States. The colonial powers of Europe could well
appreciate an educational philosophy that stood for docility,
heightened efficiency, and black subordination to white. In the
colonization of Africa, both Europeans and Americans put industrial schooling to effective use.

However, the earliest interest in the possibility for the adoption of industrial education in Africa was shown by a black man.
As early as 1879 Edward Wilmot Blyden, the Pan-Africanist,
was giving serious consideration to implementing Hampton-type
programs in the curriculum of his Liberia College. Blyden's
idea received only favorable responses from the forces of American industrial schooling. Samuel Chapman Armstrong advised
him that the industrial idea of schooling was what Africans
needed whether they were native-born Africans or of African

descent born in the United States. Hampton-type schooling, he explained to Blyden, would help set the Liberian "right side up, and do good work for that country."[1]

Blyden failed to discern the actual contradictions between the goals of industrial education and African autonomy. Like many others, he was unable to see beyond the Armstrong, Booker T. Washington rhetoric of self-help. In 1882, after he had seen Tuskegee Institute and had paid a second visit to its parent institution, Hampton, Blyden announced his intention to initiate industrial schooling at Liberia College.[2]

Other Pan-Africanists were likewise fooled by the Tuskegee image of self-help. With its black principal and all-black staff, Tuskegee seemed a fine example of black autonomy. Little did most Pan-Africanists realize that the monies that gave Tuskegee life and lifted it to prominence came from whites rather than blacks. Casely Hayford, the Gold Coast nationalist, saw a spur to "African nationality" in the accomplishments of Tuskegee Institute.[3] E. D. Morel, who had gained a reputation in his criticism of European exploitation in the Congo, called for African solidarity and Tuskegee-type education to make that goal a reality.[4] Members of the African Nationalist Congress of South Africa thought that industrial education, if adopted, could be an important force in the liberation of African people.[5] Marcus Garvey had found Washington's *Up From Slavery* a great inspiration and Tuskegee Institute a source of black pride. Garvey regretted for many years the fact that he had arrived in the United States after Washington's death and was therefore deprived of conferring with the noted founder.[6] Harry Thuku, the Kenyan labor leader, caught the essence of much of the Pan-African enthusiasm for Booker Washington's school when he credited Tuskegee as being an example of "black defiance" to white rule.[7]

W.E.B. Du Bois, however, perceptively criticized industrial education and the accommodationism of Washington in his essay, "Of Mr. Booker T. Washington and Others," which appeared in his famous work, *The Souls of Black Folk* (1903). But African leaders failed to heed its warning. Perhaps if Du Bois had spelled out his criticism of industrial education from a distinctively Pan-African perspective—that is, with specific reference to its potential danger to Africa—African leaders might have been receptive to his criticisms.

Familiarity with the American scene could make the Pan-Africanist change his opinion. The African leaders who praised Tuskegee did not understand Tuskegee. Only a few of them had visited the United States. After spending five years in America, Marcus Garvey changed his opinion. He began to understand the accommodationism that was the basis of the industrial education idea. Garvey concluded: "We have been misrepresented by our leadership. We have been taught to beg rather than to make demands. Booker T. Washington was not a leader of the Negro race. We do not look to Tuskegee. The world has recognized him as a leader, but we do not. We are going to make demands."[8]

It was easy for the colonial powers of Africa to relish a philosophy of education and life that stood for black acquiescence and obedience to the status quo. Tuskegee students, or "Captains of Industry" as Booker T. Washington liked to call them, were welcomed in Colonial Nigeria, the Belgian Congo, South Africa, and throughout British East Africa in the early twentieth century. The Germans utilized Tuskegee students as technical assistants in the development of cotton culture in Togo. The success of the Togo project made the German colonizers seriously think in 1904 of implementing industrial-type schooling on a larger basis. "The Germans have been so strongly impressed with the effects of industrial training upon the natives," Washington said, "that they have decided to introduce into all the schools of that colony [Togo] a system for the training of boys in handwork."[9]

The adoption of industrial education throughout Africa was given a big push from Americans interested in the stabilization of a world order based on white rule. Robert E. Park, the University of Chicago trained sociologist, was one of Booker Washington's most trusted white advisors and an advocate of more formal industrial education relations between Tuskegee and Africa. Park's interest in Africa had come from his study of race relations and cultural contacts on a worldwide basis. His desire to apply the industrial education formula to the African scene evolved from his commitment to historical method and cross-cultural analysis. Park saw the "Negro problem" in the United States "as an aspect or a phase of the native problem" in Africa; it was "a problem which, like slavery, had arisen as an incident in an historical process and as a phase of the natural history of civilization."[10] In his interpretation of the world order, Park held that changes would occur, but within clearly defined limits. He contended that American blacks, like their African brethren, were living in a naturally ordered world. Thus, the effect of Park's writings and teachings, as Gunnar Myrdal pointed out, was to give scientific justification to the Southern racial system.[11] And at the same time, he gave philosophical legitimacy to the application of industrial education in Colonial Africa. For Africa he recommended "education . . . that would prepare not merely the native but the European invaders, as well, for the kind of world in which they were both inescapably destined to live."[12]

Like Park, Thomas Jesse Jones envisioned a world order premised on black subordination to white. But he differed from Robert E. Park, for he turned his thoughts into action. Born in Wales and educated primarily in the American South, Jones became dedicated to the industrial education idea during his affiliation with Hampton Institute. At the end of World War I, he became a staunch internationalist like many other Europeans and Americans. Jones understood the relationship between international alliance and foreign goodwill. Certainly, the colonial powers could use assistance. Africans were discontent under colonial rule, and the growing surge of Pan-African agitation in 1919 led by Du Bois, Garvey, and others served only to stimulate the unrest.[13] Jones believed that industrial schooling could be used to strengthen America's foreign alliances by helping the colonial powers stabilize the African situation. As Kenneth James King in his study of African education noted, Jones's efforts constituted "in East Africa . . . and by determined campaigns for industrial schools in parts of West Africa, an attempt . . . to reverse the pattern of African aspirations."[14]

His efforts were not needed in French Africa, but they were

in British Africa. The French had a strong centralized program of education in their colonies, a uniformity of curriculum, and programs and teaching methods that worked well in their behalf. In marked contrast, the British lacked a centralized program. Education in the British colonies had been basically left up to the efforts of various missionary groups, with the end result that there was no uniformity of programs or educational direction. Consequently, education in British Africa was not being effectively utilized as an aid to colonization.[15] The type of education that Jones spoke of offered both uniformity and effective purpose. At the invitation of the crown, he made his first thrust into Africa in 1920 heading a special commission to examine education in British West Africa.

The efforts of Thomas Jesse Jones and his commission were well received by the British. The Colonial Office was thoroughly impressed and expressed "keen appreciation" for the commission's value.[16] Quite predictably, Jones and his group had advised the British officials that an educational program similar to that of Hampton and Tuskegee should be initiated in their colonies.[17] Of even less surprise was the commission's open endorsement of colonialism. As Jones put it: "Civilization is the result of contacts and as the people of Africa have contact with other peoples of the world so will they share in the benefits of civilization. We left West Africa with a very sincere gratitude for the great accomplishments of the British Empire in Africa."[18] The desire of the commission to aid colonization so enthused the British that Jones and his followers were invited to conduct a similar survey of British East Africa.[19]

The Phelps-Stokes Fund was an important supportive agent behind the Jones Commission to West Africa, but with the success of the first commission, more powerful forces began to commit themselves to the spreading of industrial education abroad. With the end of World War I, the Rockefeller organization began to show a greater interest in international affairs. In 1920, the Rockefeller-sponsored General Education Board formed a special subsidiary board to spearhead the organization's concern at the international level. Thus the International Education Board (IEB) was founded. Most of the members of this board served simultaneously on the General Education Board, including IEB President Wickliffe Rose. The success of the Jones Commission in West Africa and the invitation by the British for the commission to conduct a survey of East Africa gave the IEB the perfect opportunity to launch into the international scene in support of white-ruled world order through international black industrial education. Anson Phelps Stokes wrote to Wickliffe Rose, saying that he understood that Rose and "associate officers were present at the week-end conference . . . when the policy of some of the Rockefeller Boards was under consideration, discussed the proposed Commission to East Africa" and were "so much interested in it" that they would "recommend at the next meeting of the International Education Board that a sum of three thousand dollars be placed at the disposal of the Phelps-Stokes Trustees," to be expended in connection with the proposed survey.[20] The IEB's interest was greater than three thousand dollars. The board resolved at its meeting of November 19, 1923, "that the sum of six thousand dollars ($6,000) be, and it is hereby, appropriated to the Phelps-Stokes Fund to be used toward defraying the expenses of an Educational Commission to East Africa."[21]

Having the Rockefeller organization and the crown behind the commission, however, did nothing to change the fact that Jones and his followers would have to prove themselves to the white settler population of East Africa. Arriving in Kenya in 1923, the commission was met with suspicion by the local whites. They had apprehensions about the nature of the proposed survey and those conducting it. Thomas Jesse Jones explained that the commission was in sympathy with the goals of colonialism and that the group's report would benefit the colonists by providing them with usable information and recommendations.

Jones referred to the commission as well balanced, with men who could relate to the problems of the colonists and work within the status quo. "Dr. James Hardy Dillard is by birth from the southern part of the United States," he informed a white audience in Nairobi, "the section where there are many negroes and the section where slavery formerly prevailed. . . .

His approach is not that of the outside, theoretical, idealism but the result of a lifetime spent with black people working as labourers on farms, etc." Jones concluded in his portrait of Dr. Dillard, "we feel that here in Kenya he will be able to understand the problems of Native education from a very sympathetic and constructive attitude."[22]

The commission's only black member, Dr. James Emman Kwegyir Aggrey, was a man in whom the colonial whites should have found no faults. It may well be argued that Aggrey was the Booker T. Washington of Africa. Jones considered him "the most interesting member of" their "whole party." Dr. Aggrey, a native-born African who had received his education in the United States, believed that progress for Africans was dependent on the good graces of the colonial powers. He advocated mutual prosperity with social inequality and the "right kind" of education for Africans. As Aggrey said before a white South African audience: "This country has wonderful possibilities and we want you to make us assets instead of liabilities. We want education of the mind, of the heart and of the hand—the mind to lead, the hand to do, and the heart to touch it all with immortality."[23] In impressing upon the colonial whites of Kenya the suitability of Aggrey for the task at hand, Jones noted that the whites of South Africa had found him acceptable. "When he went to South Africa they were, of course, rather dubious of Africans with American education," Jones remarked, "but General Smuts and others were so impressed by his constructive attitude that they offered him a position to remain there permanently as Master of Native Studies!"[24]

In addition, Jones and his group boasted of their commitment to the Lugardian philosophy of education for the natives. Frederick Lugard, the architect of "indirect rule" in Africa, professed that native education was an essential ingredient for the propagation of colonialism. Lugard contended that the "primary function of education should . . . be to fit the ordinary individual to fill a useful part in his environment . . . and to ensure that the exceptional individual shall use his abilities for the advancement of the community and not . . . to the subversion of constituted authority."[25] This idea was represented within the commission in the person of Major Hans Vischer, Secretary of the British Advisory Committee on Education in Africa and former Director of Education in Nigeria. Vischer had worked under Lugard and had earned the reputation as one of the ablest proponents of Lugardian theory and colonial rule.[26]

The commission was in complete philosophical accord with colonization. They traveled throughout the colonies, endorsing colonialism in Kenya, Uganda, Tanzania, Zanzibar, Nyasaland, Sierra Leone, Gold Coast, Nigeria, sections of South Africa, and finally in Southern Rhodesia, where they took part in the Missionary Conference on Education. His Excellency the Governor of Southern Rhodesia addressed the crowd and gave a heartfelt greeting to the commission members present. The governor expressed his concern over how best to assure white rule. "We are a population of 40,000 Europeans, living among twenty times that number of natives. How to ensure the continuance of happy relations between a highly civilised race and a primitive race living alongside one another is a question that bristles with difficulties." The governor claimed that the colonist felt paternalistic toward the Africans: "We are in our African Colonies the trustees of the backward and primitive indigenous races; and that it is our solemn duty to protect them from outside enemies and from themselves, and to do all that we can to promote their moral, intellectual and material welfare." The task ahead, he contended, was much easier than what Macaulay faced in trying to introduce Western education into India, because the natives of Southern Rhodesia were "without civilisation and with traditions that go little further back than the memories of the oldest inhabitant."[27]

The governor reiterated the need for a type of education that abided by the prejudices of the ruling class. He contended that the two races were totally unable to meet on a social level, and beyond that, should be kept separated as much as possible:

> There is, I believe, no difference of opinion among
> those who have knowledge and experience of this
> country that some measure of segregation is essen-

tial to the comfort and happiness of Europeans and natives alike; and to the maintenance of that good-will between the two races, which I am glad to think prevails in Southern Rhodesia at the present time.[28]

On the other hand, however, he believed that complete seg-regation was impossible to maintain and "impractical." The basis of this impracticality was the country's need for and de-pendence on black labor. Blacks were essential to the prosper-ity of Southern Rhodesia, and for this reason the governor ad-vocated that the two races be kept separated socially but united on all matters of mutual progress. To remove blacks from con-tact with whites completely, he admitted, "would be econom-ically disastrous."[29]

The best possible solution would be the remedy that would lead blacks into harmless social channels and at the same time increase their economic value. This formulation had been most clearly worked out in the American experiment in education for Southern blacks initiated at Hampton and Tuskegee. The governor recommended industrial education for the natives of Southern Rhodesia. He advised those who thought that indus-trial schooling meant training Africans for skilled positions not to worry: "It need not be assumed that in the immediate future, and indeed for generations to come, the native with his inferior mental development will be able to compete seriously with the white artisan." He suggested that through industrial education blacks might be given the "elementary handicrafts" that would make them more valuable to the country, to them-selves, and at the same time "minimise the danger of econom-ic rivalry between the two races."[30]

Thomas Jesse Jones applauded the governor's faith in indus-trial education and hailed his entire message as "perfectly won-derful." "You are most fortunate that you have a Governor of that calibre here," he told the Southern Rhodesian audience gathered at the Missionary Conference, "—a Governor who stated the problems so clearly and with such definiteness and who has not dodged any part of them." Jones admitted that he and the other members of the Commission on East African Education felt that "the British Empire . . . was one of the great agencies of God for the establishment of righteousness upon earth. (Prolonged applause)."[31]

The Commission on East African Education and the ideas it espoused gained wide acceptance. Thomas Jesse Jones reported to Wickliffe Rose in October 1924: "The co-operation of Government, missions and settlers has exceeded our expectations in kindness."[32] The British found the industrial-type schooling perfectly suitable to their needs. Jones told Rose: "The interest of the British Government in the enlargement of their educational activities along practical lines is quite remarkable."[33] The Colonial Office Advisory Committee on Education began meeting on a regular basis to "consider the application of the Colonies for authority and aid to change their educational system" to an industrial education one.[34]

Their interest led to concrete action. The British saw the potential of industrial schooling for incorporation into their colonial structure. The British Empire Advisory Committee on Education reported: "There is obviously an intimate connection between educational policy and the economic development of a territory. Educational policy must be planned with reference to the kind of life the pupils may be expected to lead. . . ." This process could be carried out in an inexpensive fashion, as the Southern states in America had demonstrated. "The right kind of organization and the right methods of propaganda," the committee concluded, "may achieve much with comparatively small expenditure."[35] J. H. Oldham, Secretary of the International Missionary Council and a staunch advocate of applying the industrial schooling idea to Africa, notified the IEB and the Phelps-Stokes Fund in January of 1925: "The educational reports of the . . . Commissions to West Africa and to East Africa have laid the basis for government programs in education in the various African colonies. The Colonial Office is taking the matter up with earnestness."[36] Indeed, the British Colonial Office wished to become as familiar as possible with the work of Hampton and Tuskegee by sending representatives to the American South. Anson Phelps Stokes said that for the British to have their "leaders in governmental and missionary education see for themselves what is being done in the matter of Negro education, especially in agricultural and industrial . . . will insure the adoption of *wise* [italics mine] policies in matters of Negro education in most of the African colonies."[37]

The decision by the British to implement industrial-type schooling signaled the beginning of a formal policy of educational cooperation between the American crusaders for industrial education and the colonizers of Africa. Colonial governments began sending some of their officers to study educational developments in the Southern regions of the United States. The Commission on East African Education wished Dr. C. T. Loram to visit America to examine firsthand the work of the various black industrial schools. Loram, who served as Chairman of the South African Native Affairs Commission, was in favor of utilizing industrial schooling to solve the "Native problem" in South Africa. Jesse Jones beseeched the Phelps-Stokes Fund and the International Education Board to sponsor Loram's trip. Anson Phelps Stokes wrote to Wickliffe Rose:

> As you know, Dr. Loram is the leading authority in South Africa on the education of the blacks and is the most influential member of the Native Affairs Commission, appointed by the Government. Dr. Loram planned to come to America this winter, but owing to the change of Government, the new Premier [General Hertzog of the Nationalist Regime] felt it important that he should be in South Africa to aid him in formulating wise policies.[38]

However, Loram would be free to come to the United States sometime that winter, and the Phelps-Stokes Fund was prepared to appropriate five hundred dollars toward his trip. The bulk of the expenses would have to be borne by the IEB. Rose commented that the International Education Board was thoroughly elated over the idea of having Loram come to America, but since this was somewhat unusual, they would have to take the matter up with the board's financial backers.[39]

The request by Jones that Loram and other "African educators" be brought to the United States to see the industrial schools resulted in producing the one incident in which the IEB disclosed the real throne of power behind the board. The matter of funds for the trips was somewhat out of the board's usual character and, therefore, had to be taken up with a higher source. Wickliffe Rose wrote to John D. Rockefeller, Jr.:

> Since a request of this kind [sponsoring Loram and other African educators to visit America] lies outside the present field of activities of the International Education Board, the officers would not care to present it unless it should meet with your personal approval. With that approval, however, we should be disposed to recommend it.[40]

Rockefeller gave his verbal approval of the proposal.[41]

Dr. Loram came to the United States in 1926 with the hope of finding the solution to the "native problem." He was a "unique" man, as Jesse Jones had promised. His uniqueness stemmed from his ability to assess the South African situation from a perspective which, according to him, would benefit both Africans and whites. His belief: "Segregation The Key To Solution."[42] Loram advocated that the whites and Africans of South Africa remain separated at all costs. He considered segregation to be natural. The South African Land Act of 1913 was to him the best way of insuring the "destiny of South Africa." That act confined blacks to "reserves" to guarantee that the two races remain segregated. Of course, it left the Europeans with 90 percent of the habitable land of South Africa and all the country's mineral resources. The situation in South Africa became more intense with the passing of each day as African discontent with the reserves (or concentration camps) increased. The dominant factor behind Loram's visit to the United States was to explore possibilities that might aid the segregation policy of South Africa and make it more workable. He confided to members of the Phelps-Stokes Fund and the International Education Board that the South African native situation was "growingly serious."[43]

A contributing factor to white uneasiness in South Africa was the Garvey movement.[44] Garveyism had gained an immense following in the 1920s throughout Black America and Africa. The South African white population dreaded his philosophy of nationalism with its pronouncement of "Africa for Africans." They had much to fear, since they were a ruling minority whose subjects outnumbered them twenty to one. Loram was one of the leading propagandists against Garveyism. "The ravings of Garveyism . . . should not be allowed to disturb us," he proclaimed in his effort to console his fellow whites of South Africa. He added, "The people of the negro Republic, Liberia, would not admit Garvey or his following."[45]

But the white population of South Africa remained concerned about the impact of Garveyism and other efforts at black self-assertion. Loram did admit that South Africa had been "startled" by Garvey and his professed "anti-Europeanism and non-cooperation."[46] Loram contended that the African population wanted to cooperate and should be given more inducements to do so. Like other whites, he had felt the power of Clement Kadalie's agitation for unionism among African workers. Along with the discontent Africans were demonstrating over the reserves system, Garveyism caused many whites of South Africa to rethink their strategy on the African.

How to insure that the African would remain humble, docile, nonpolitical and unorganized was the question to which Loram believed he found the answer in the United States. "The native was a cheerful worker," Loram said, "and only those who had worked with Indians could appreciate him. There was no reason why he should not continue to work as he had worked in the past."[47] Loram contended that "proper" education for the African was the key, and in America's South he saw an idea working that he considered applicable to the South African situation. He announced at a dinner held in his honor by the IEB and the Phelps-Stokes Fund, "I have seen many remarkable things in the South. I have admired the 'finish' of Hampton. I have seen the greatness of Tuskegee. . . . I believe I have found the ideal school and the model for African education."[48] (See the Appendix.)

By 1927, the industrial education idea had gained a long list of subscribers that included: the British Colonial Office, British universities and schools, the Belgian Colonial Office, the Belgian Red Cross, the French Colonial Office, the Portuguese Colonial Representative, the Mission Societies of America and Europe, and through Dr. Loram, South Africa. Although only the British readily moved to adopt industrial schooling throughout its colonies, all others at least implemented it on a limited scale.[49]

The industrial education idea was utilized in America's own colonization effort in Africa. Liberia was an unofficial colony of America, acquired in the nineteenth century. Its destiny was inextricably linked to that of the United States when, in the 1820s, the American Colonization Society designated it as the site for the relocation of American blacks on the African continent. The tiny country had received only scant attention until its mineral resource potential was realized in the twentieth century. Liberia was rich in palm oil, cocoa, coffee, black gum, mahogany, cherry, peach, iron wood, and other fine lumbers, but most of all, rubber. And when in 1926 Harvey Firestone established his rubber plantation in Liberia, this seemed to signal the go-ahead for a resurgence of American activity in the area. The crusaders for industrial education moved to aid in the colonization of Liberia.

The International Education Board and the Phelps-Stokes Fund came together to back Thomas Jesse Jones in the revival of the New York Colonization Society (NYCS), which had been an auxiliary of the American Colonization Society. The NYCS would serve as a supportive agency to America's new thrust into Liberia. The NYCS was under the supervision of Jones and Jackson Davis. Its rebirth had been inspired by the growth in popularity across the world of the industrial education idea, an idea most suitable for the heightened exploitation of Liberia's resource potential. In 1928, the NYCS sent a commission to Liberia to find a suitable site for establishing an industrial school. The country had three educational institutions: the College of Liberia, supported by the Liberian Government, the College of West Africa, which was supported by the Methodist Board, and Monrovia College, which was supported by the African Methodists. But none was exclusively "industrial." The NYCS Commission to Liberia reported that it found a desperate need for Hampton-Tuskegee education in the country. "As I have observed it," R. R. Taylor, head of the commission, said, "Liberia with a few exceptions such as the Firestone plantations has very little agriculture, little organized industry. . . . I am therefore recommending that the site at Kakata be selected for the [industrial] school location."[50]

The school would aid in the exploitation of Liberian rubber. The site at Kakata was selected not because of its close proximity to the capital city of Liberia, Monrovia, nor because the area with its ridges separated by rather shallow ravines "resembled in a way the contour at Tuskegee," but because it would be near the Firestone plantations.[51]

That the school and the Firestone rubber works would have a firm relationship is clear from the proposed course of study at "Booker T. Washington Agricultural and Industrial Institute of Liberia." Within its industrial framework the school would emphasize agricultural work with

> special emphasis on a course which for want of a
> better name might be termed "Forest Trees." Much
> of the wealth of the country is bound up in the trees,
> the rubber. . . . These trees have all the highest commercial value, and such a course would include not
> only a study of the trees themselves and their products but particularly methods of improving the product and increasing the yield.[52]

The end result would be rich dividends to all concerned, or so Taylor maintained.

The benefit to the African laborer, however, was not a consideration. The course of training proposed at Booker Washington Institute promised greater utilization of native labor, but not that the native would be elevated to the highest skill positions. Those positions were reserved for the plantations' white labor force. The Firestone organization was primarily concerned with making the native labor "more efficient" in the planting of the rubber trees and in the harvesting of the rubber. Taylor noted that if the men became more proficient, the commercial return would be phenomenal. Donald Ross, the efficiency manager of the Firestone plantations, confided to him "that one hundred acres planted in rubber trees would yield when in bearing a net profit of five thousand dollars ($5,000) per year at the present price of rubber; from eighty to one hundred trees" might be planted to each acre and "one person" well educated could "attend four acres."[53]

Training at Booker Washington Institute aimed at making the Liberian men more efficient laborers and the women supportive agents for efficiency. As the crusaders for industrial education saw them, the Liberian women were necessary only in terms of their contribution to the heightened proficiency and stabilization of the male workers. "The work for girls is of the utmost importance and presents problems which are difficult and perplexing," Taylor declared. "Naturally, it should center around the home. . . . The educational system of Liberia will expand, requiring more trained workers and the young men who are being educated will want trained help-meets to establish more stable and attractive homes." He contended, therefore, that the course of study for the women at Booker Washington Institute should consist of "Sewing," "Cooking," "Laundrying," "Care of Children," "Home Gardening," and "Housekeeping."[54]

The molding of character traits conducive to better labor would constitute a central role in the institute's program for both men and women. The educational crusaders considered religion to be of central importance for this purpose. "Along with all this training of the mind and hand," Taylor and associates contended, "should go religious teaching. Whatever else may be accomplished woud lose much of its value unless there was a solid basis of religion. . . ." Like the Hampton and Tuskegee models, devotional exercises, prayer meetings, "and other forms of religious service would be part of the daily program."[55]

Utmost to the success of an educational program is its faculty, and the promoters of Booker T. Washington Agricultural and Industrial Institute (BWI) of Liberia picked the type of pedagogues most suited for the work at hand. They needed rugged individuals who were able to take on the challenges of a pioneering venture and fitted to the educational philosophy and methods. The New York Colonization Society was, in short, looking for "good colored" men "for the Booker Washington Institute in Liberia."[56] They had to search no further than the ranks of Hampton and Tuskegee graduates. These schools provided BWI with its teaching staff throughout the duration of the institute.[57]

The choice for a principal of the Booker Washington Institute was a different matter altogether. The New York Colonization Society, the Phelps-Stokes Fund and the International Education Board all agreed that they needed a man well grounded in the industrial education idea, preferably someone who had taught or administrated over one of the industrial schools of the South, a man who would convey the proper image to Africans. Their thinking was like that of Thomas Jesse Jones and Jackson Davis, "that the principal and one other man on the staff ought to be white."[58]

When Booker Washington Institute officially opened in 1929, it was under the principalship of James L. Sibley, a man in whom the crusaders for industrial education in Liberia had profound faith to carry the program through. Sibley was a Southerner, former State Agent of Negro Rural Schools in Alabama, a strong advocate of industrial schooling, and he was white. He immediately set out to bring BWI into complete harmony with the local tribes and villages and into a firm working relationship with the Firestone plantations. But he was claimed by yellow fever before he was able to put his program on solid footing.[59]

Sibley's replacement was Paul W. Rupel, a man of much the same background, who took charge with a dynamic zeal and determination to make BWI live up to its namesake, Booker T. Washington. Sibley's concern was labor and industry, pure and simple. He made a careful review of his staff, fired those who did not meet his expectations, and praised those whom he felt were doing a good job. An example of those who met his expectations was "Mr. Coles," whom he classified as a "poor classroom teacher," but in the more important category, "good at handling the natives at the rough work."[60]

Curriculum changes were made with stronger emphasis on

work in the fields. Rupel insisted that students work longer hours and that they do so no matter what the conditions. He declared that if students "did not want to work in the rain they should not come" to this institute. "They were losing so much time at this time of year [the wet season] by stopping every time it rained and the school was the loser. They work on the road for the Government and at Firestone's in the rain so they should expect to work in the rain here."[61]

Rupel was determined to produce the best workers or none at all; and as he reported to Thomas Jesse Jones, he would stick to the task until the job was done or "until snow flies at Booker Washington Institute." Rupel said he meant to "put SOUL into this Institution."[62] In one short year under his guidance, the Booker T. Washington Institute became the central institution for education in Liberia.[63] Its student body increased from sixty-eight students to over six hundred. The institution's enrollment represented most of the tribes of Liberia: the Bassa, Buzi, Kpelle, Gbande, Kru, Mano, Mandingo, Grebo, Gizi, Gola, Akra, Guio, Kwana, and Kongo all had members attending BWI. It had new dormitories, a physical plant, well-constructed housing for the faculty, a rapidly expanding library, a laboratory, tools, and machinery. The school, indeed, was developing at a fantastic rate, producing valuable laborers for the Firestone plantations.[64]

Substantial impetus for the school's growth came from the Firestone organization. It provided specialists to help erect buildings and provided machinery, tools, and just about anything else the institute required.[65] The Firestone plantations entertained all visitors to BWI on the school's behalf. When Jackson Davis came to inspect the institute, he was met at the docks by BWI and Firestone officials and, in fact, spent most of his time "inspecting the rubber" rather than examining the school.[66]

The Firestone organization and BWI maintained a close working relationship. Firestone Plantation Chief Engineer "Mr. Runnals stated that the whole staff on the Plantation are always ready and eager to assist Mr. Rupel."[67] The Firestone interests gave the school direct financial assistance. Next to the monies provided by the IEB and the Phelps-Stokes Fund (through the New York Colonization Society), Harvey Firestone was Booker Washington Institute's largest single contributor.[68] He and other crusaders for industrial schooling in Liberia vowed "that all efforts should be made to develop the Washington Institute. . . ."[69]

That the Firestones constituted a major force behind Booker Washington Institute is revealed in the "Minutes of the Meeting of the Board of Trustees of the Booker Washington Agricultural and Industrial Institute of Liberia for May 22, 1936." At that meeting the board expressed its "many thanks" to the Firestone Tire and Rubber Company for its assistance. The secretary was "requested to express to Mr. Harvey S. Firestone, Jr., the deep appreciation of the Trustees of the Booker Washington Institute for his very generous gift which also was imperative to the realization of the building and equipment program now being carried out at the Institute."[70] The board could have waited until a later date when all its members were present and thanked Mr. Firestone in person. The Board of Trustees of BWI consisted of Henry L. West, President, George G. Wolkins, Anson Phelps Stokes, Robert R. Moton (the man who succeeded Booker T. Washington as principal of Tuskegee Institute and the board's only black member), and Harvey S. Firestone, Jr.[71]

The influence of the Firestone organization in Liberia went beyond the confines of Booker Washington Institute. The school did provide more efficient workers for the Firestone plantations and served as an "example" to the natives of Firestone "goodwill,"[72] but comprised only one component of the necessary two ingredients for the organization's continued success in Liberia. The government of that country provided the other.

Edwin Barclay, President of Liberia, worked in harmony with the Firestone exploitation of his country's rubber and labor. He contended with other government officials that the Firestone plantations were good for the country. They seconded the report of the educational crusaders:

> [The Firestone Company represents] high business principles in dealing with its employees as well as with the general public. Though the purpose of the organization in Liberia is avowedly economic and

> commercial, their sound business principles and methods have been maintained in all their Liberian activities. The company has been uniformly just and generous in dealing with Native labor both as regards wages and conditions of employment. [73]

It seemed of little importance to the government that the Liberian worker on the Firestone plantations was paid one of the lowest wages in the world or that the revenue the country was supposed to receive from the harvest of the nation's rubber was based on an export tax that was also one of the lowest in the world: "1% upon the value."[74] There is good reason to believe that Jackson Davis meant more than what he wrote when he reported in confidence: "President Barclay stated that he had arrived at a satisfactory understanding with Mr. Firestone."[75]

The "understanding" between Barclay and Firestone worked to the advantage of the Firestone plantations and to the disadvantage of native labor. A few days after the meeting between the two men, President Barclay announced a road-building program. A network of improved roads was to be built—one from Monrovia through Kakata and the other from the Sierra Leone border to the Liberian coast—roads that happened to link the Firestone plantations. Moreover, the labor for the construction of these roads was conscripted and included BWI students and other natives from nearby tribes.[76]

The NYCS showed no compassion for the problems of the native workers. The natives, both students and nonstudents, raised a loud clamor that they were being enslaved for the road program. Jackson Davis took glib notice of the situation during his visit to Liberia. He reported back to the NYCS that the Africans were merely "work[ing] a month on the road in lieu of paying taxes. Some may say this is forced labor, but I see nothing to get excited about. It is the African pay-as-you-go plan."[77]

Whatever name one gave to the conscription of labor in Liberia, it was a practice that most natives felt bitter resentment about. The road-building incident induced an atmosphere of distrust between BWI students and the institute. Some felt that the institute betrayed them by supporting conscription and for not using its influence to at least have them excused from working on the road project. This air of discontent continued for three years after the 1935 road project had begun. It manifested itself in numerous ways. It was reported that students did not seem to be taking their lessons seriously; many were dropping out of the institution; and school property was being destroyed or stolen. Moreover, many local natives had never been convinced that the foreigner's institute had their best interest at heart; to them it was a place to be despised—"a place to rob and steal all you can get."[78]

The continued drop in BWI's "holding power" after 1936 led to a major conference of the crusaders for industrial education. On December 5, 1938, Thomas Jesse Jones called for a meeting to be held on December 13 for the representatives of the various boards and the Firestone Tire and Rubber Company.[79] Perhaps we may never know what was said at that final meeting. We do know that BWI was terminated shortly thereafter and that the Firestone plantations incorporated the remnants of the school into what became the company's official training program for its native laborers. Like the entire world, the educational crusaders were turning their attention to the tumultuous years of war that lay ahead.

The industrial education idea never died. It was an attractive idea to whites who held power and desired to keep that power. Thomas Jesse Jones well understood this when he said in 1940: "Little wonder is it that educators in Africa, in the Orient, in the islands of the Sea and in our own United States have looked to Hampton for ideals and methods of relating education to the common life of the common people."[80] The ideal, however, was white rule, and the method was a dissemination of educational ideas that were conducive to perpetual slavery.

NOTES

1. *Southern Workman,* February 1880, p. 9.

2. Ibid., January 1883, p. 9; Hollis R. Lynch, *Edward Wilmot Blyden* (London: Oxford University Press, 1967), p. 115.

3. Kenneth James King, *Pan-Africanism and Education: A Study of Race Philanthropy and Education in the Southern States of America and East Africa* (London: Oxford University Press, 1971), p. 17.

4. E. D. Morel, "The Future of Tropical Africa," *Southern Workman*, June 1912, pp. 353-354.

5. Manning Marable, "Booker T. Washington and African Nationalism," *Phylon* 35:4 (1974), p. 398. See also Louis R. Harlan, "Booker T. Washington and the White Man's Burden," *American Historical Review* 81 (January 1966), pp. 441-467.

6. Theodore G. Vincent, *Black Power and The Garvey Movement* (San Francisco: Ramparts, 1972), p. 26.

7. King, p. 76.

8. Cited in Vincent, p. 26.

9. Booker T. Washington, *Working With the Hands* (New York: Doubleday, 1904), p. 230.

10. Robert E. Park, "Founder's Day Address, Tuskegee Institute, April 12, 1942," Tuskegee Institute Library; Fred H. Matthews, "Robert Park, Congo Reform and Tuskegee: The Molding of a Race Relations Expert, 1905-1913," *Canadian Journal of History: Annales Canadiennes D'Histoire* 8, no. 1 (March 1973), p. 41.

11. Gunnar Myrdal, *An American Dilemma: The Negro Problem and Modern Democracy*, Vol. 2 (New York: Harper and Row, 1944), p. 1362; Matthews, p. 65.

12. Park, "Founder's Day Address, Tuskegee Institute, April 12, 1942," p. 3.

13. W.E.B. Du Bois, *The World and Africa* (New York: International Publishers, 1946), pp. 8-12; For further discussion, see Kwame Nkrumah, *Africa Must Unite* (New York: International Publishers, 1963); Chancellor Williams, *The Destruction of Black Civilization* (Chicago: Third World Press, 1974), pp. 337-340; and Walter Rodney, *How Europe Underdeveloped Africa* (Washington, D.C.: Howard University Press, 1974), pp. 205-281.

14. King, p. 257. For further discussion, see Philip J. Foster, *Education and Social Change in Ghana* (Chicago: University of Chicago Press, 1965), Chapter 5, and L. J. Lewis, *The Phelps-Stokes Reports on Education in Africa* (London: Oxford University Press, 1962).

15. Remi Clignet, "Assimilation in African Education," *Journal of Modern African Studies* 8:3 (1970), pp. 427-431.

16. Memo to Anson Phelps Stokes, 21 September 1923, *International Education Board Collection*, File No. 221, Rockefeller Archives.

17. Thomas Jesse Jones, *Education in Africa: A Study of West, South, and Equatorial Africa* (London: Edinburgh House Press, 1922).

18. "You Will Solve Your Problems All Right," *East African Standard*, Nairobi, Kenya, 3 March 1924, p. 1.

19. Memo to Anson Phelps Stokes, 21 September 1923, *International Education Board Collection*, File No. 22.

20. Anson Phelps Stokes to Wickliffe Rose, 2 October 1923, *International Education Board Collection*, File No. 221, Rockefeller Archives.

21. Wickliffe Rose to Thomas Jesse Jones, 21 November 1923, *International Education Board Collection*, File No. 221.

22. *East African Standard*, 25 February 1924, p. 2.

23. Ibid., 3 March 1924, p. 1.

24. Ibid., 25 February 1924, p. 2.

25. Margery Freda Perham, *Lugard: The Years of Adventure* (London: Collins, 1956), p. 491.

26. *East African Standard*, 25 February 1924, p. 2.

27. Clippings from the *Rhodesia Herald*, 2 June 1924, *International Education Board Collection*, File No. 221.

28. Ibid.

29. Ibid.

30. Ibid.

31. Ibid.

32. Thomas Jesse Jones to Wickliffe Rose, 9 October 1924, *International Education Board Collection*, File No. 221, p. 1.

33. Thomas Jesse Jones to Wickliffe Rose, 18 December 1924, *International Education Board Collection*, File No. 221, p. 1.

34. Ibid.

35. Extracts from Memorandum of British Empire Advisory Committee on Education 1935, *International Education Board Collection*, File No. 221, p. 2.

36. J. H. Oldham to Phelps-Stokes Fund, 21 January 1925, *International Education Board Collection*, File No. 221, p. 1.

37. Anson Phelps Stokes to Wickliffe Rose, 21 October 1924, *International Education Board Collection*, File No. 221, p. 2.

38. Anson Phelps Stokes to Wickliffe Rose, 16 October 1924, *International Education Board Collection*, File No. 221, p. 1.

39. Anson Phelps Stokes to Wickliffe Rose, 17 October 1924, Wickliffe Rose to Thomas Jesse Jones, 20 October 1924, *International Education Board Collection*, File No. 221.

40. Wickliffe Rose to John D. Rockefeller, Jr., 6 November 1924, *International Education Board Collection*, File No. 221.

41. Memo from Rose to his secretary to "kindly keep the letter in the files, with this note, as a matter of record that Mr. Rockefeller gave his verbal approval of the proposal." Memo dated 8 November 1924,

International Education Board Collection, File No. 221.

42. Newspaper clippings dated December 1924, found in *International Education Board Collection*, File No. 221.

43. Ibid.

44. Ibid.

45. Ibid.

46. Ibid.

47. Ibid.

48. "Address By Dr. C. T. Loram on the Native Affairs Commission, Union of South Africa, on the Occasion of a Dinner Given in his Honour," dated January 4, 1927, *International Education Board Collection*, File No. 221, p. 4.

49. Ibid.; Extracts from Memorandum of British Empire Advisory Committee on Education 1935, *International Education Board Collection*, File No. 221. See also Thomas Jesse Jones, *Education in East Africa: A Study of East, Central and South Africa* (London: Edinburgh House Press, 1925).

50. Report of R. R. Taylor upon the Booker Washington Agricultural and Industrial Institute at Kakata, Republic of Liberia, October 1929, *International Education Board Collection*, File No. 290: Booker T. Washington Agricultural and Industrial Institute (BWI) of Liberia, p. 6.

51. Ibid., pp. 4-5; Report on Educational Needs and Opportunities in Liberia, undated, *International Education Board Collection*, File No. 290: BWI of Liberia, p. 7.

52. Report of R. R. Taylor upon the Booker Washington Agricultural and Industrial Institutes at Kakata, Republic of Liberia, October 1929, p. 8.

53. Ibid.

54. Ibid., p. 11.

55. Ibid., p. 12.

56. Arthur D. Wright to Jackson Davis, 13 March 1939, *International Education Board Collection*, File No. 290: BWI of Liberia.

57. Ibid.; Jackson Davis to Arthur Wright, 15 March 1939; Memo to Jackson Davis, 19 August 1936; Leo M. Favrot to Thomas Jesse Jones, 6 March 1935, *International Education Board Collection*, File No. 290: BWI of Liberia.

58. Confidential memo to members of the New York Colonization Society, "Impressions of Liberia—March 31-April 12, 1935," *International Education Board Collection*, File No. 290: BWI of Liberia, p. 2.

59. Report on Educational Needs and Opportunities in Liberia, undated, *International Education Board Collection*, File No. 290: BWI of Liberia, p. 2.

60. Paul W. Rupel to Thomas Jesse Jones, 26 September 1935, *Inter-*

national Education Board Collection, File No. 290: BWI of Liberia, p. 2.

61. Ibid., p. 3.

62. Ibid., p. 5.

63. Memorandum from Thomas Jesse Jones to Jackson Davis, 26 March 1936, *International Education Board Collection*, File No. 290: BWI of Liberia.

64. Ibid.; Paul W. Rupel to Thomas Jesse Jones, 26 September 1935, ibid.

65. Report on Educational Needs and Opportunities in Liberia, undated, pp. 1, 5; Memo from Jackson Davis to Thomas Jesse Jones, 15 April 1935, pp. 1, 4-7; Mrs. Paul Rupel to Thomas Jesse Jones, 13 February 1936, pp. 1-2; Legation of the United States of America, Monrovia, Liberia, to Jackson Davis, 7 September 1935, pp. 1-4; *International Education Board Collection*, File No. 290: BWI of Liberia.

66. Jackson Davis to Thomas Jesse Jones, 15 April 1935, *International Education Board Collection*, File No. 290: BWI of Liberia, pp. 1-7.

67. "Minutes of the Meeting of the Board of Trustees of the Booker Washington Agricultural and Industrial Institute of Liberia, 22 May 1936," *International Education Board Collection*, File No. 290: BWI of Liberia, p. 4.

68. Report on Educational Needs and Opportunities in Liberia, undated, pp. 1, 5; Memo from Jackson Davis to Thomas Jesse Jones, 15 April 1935, pp. 1, 4-7; Mrs. Paul Rupel to Thomas Jesse Jones, 13 February 1936, pp. 1-2; Legation of the United States of America, Monrovia, Liberia, to Jackson Davis, 7 September 1935, pp. 1-4; *International Education Board Collection*, File No. 290: BWI of Liberia.

69. Memorandum from Thomas Jesse Jones to Jackson Davis, 26 March 1936, *International Education Board Collection*, File No. 290: BWI of Liberia, p. 3.

70. "Minutes of the Meeting of the Board of Trustees of the Booker Washington Agricultural and Industrial Institute of Liberia, 22 May 1936," *International Education Board Collection*, File No. 290: BWI of Liberia, p. 2.

71. Ibid., p. 1.

72. Report on Educational Needs and Opportunities in Liberia, undated, pp. 4, 8; Thomas Jesse Jones to Harvey S. Firestone, Jr., 5 December 1938, pp. 1-2; *International Education Board Collection*, File No. 290: BWI of Liberia.

73. "Liberia and the League of Nations," Address by Thomas Jesse Jones at the League of Nations Association Convention, St. Louis, Missouri, 13 January 1933, *International Education Board Collection*, File No. 290: BWI of Liberia, p. 3.

74. Report on Educational Needs and Opportunities in Liberia, un-

dated, *International Education Board Collection,* File No. 290: BWI of Liberia, p. 1.

75. Confidential memo to members of the New York Colonization Society, "Impressions of Liberia—March 31-April 12, 1935," *International Education Board Collection,* File No. 290: BWI of Liberia, p. 1.

76. Ibid., p. 2.

77. Ibid.

78. Paul W. Rupel to Thomas Jesse Jones, 26 September 1935, *International Education Board Collection,* File No. 290: BWI of Liberia, p. 5.

79. Thomas Jesse Jones to Harvey S. Firestone, 5 December 1938, *International Educational Board Collection,* File No. 290: BWI of Liberia.

80. Thomas Jesse Jones, "Hampton Institute and Dr. Malcolm Maclean," Founder's Day Address, Hampton Institute, 1940, *General Education Board Papers,* File No. Va 38, Series 1, Box 176, p. 2, Rockefeller Archives.

APPENDIX

GUESTS AT THE DINNER HELD IN HONOR
OF CHARLES T. LORAM AT THE
HOTEL ASTOR, NEW YORK, OCTOBER 25, 1926

Dr. Arthur J. Brown, Secretary of the Presbyterian Board of Foreign Missions.

Mrs. Arthur J. Brown.

Dr. Elmer Ellsworth Brown, Chancellor of New York University.

Dr. Otis Caldwell, Principal of the Lincoln School, New York City.

Mr. Thomas S. Donohugh, Secretary of the Foreign Missions Board of the Methodist Episcopal Church.

Dr. Stephen P. Duggan, Director of the International Institute of Education.

Mr. John R. Edwards, Corresponding Secretary of the Methodist Board of Foreign Missions.

Mr. Edwin R. Embree, Secretary of the Rockefeller Foundation.

Mr. Clark Foreman, Assistant to the Director, Phelps-Stokes Fund.

Mr. Clyde Furst, Secretary of the Carnegie Foundation.

Dr. George E. Haynes, Secretary of the Commission on Inter-Racial Relations, Federal Council of Churches.

Mr. John Sherman Hoyt, Trustee of the Phelps-Stokes Fund.

Dr. Mordecai Johnson, President of Howard University, Washington, D.C.

Mrs. Thomas Jesse Jones.

Dr. F. P. Keppel, President of the Carnegie Corporation.

Mr. A. E. LeRoy, Principal of the Amanzimtoti Institute, Durban, Natal.

Dr. P.H.J. Lerrigo, Secretary of the Baptist Foreign Missions Board.

Mr. Robert M. Lester, Assistant to the President, Carnegie Corporation.

Dr. C. T. Loram, Member of Native Affairs, Commission of the Union of South Africa.

Mrs. C. T. Loram.

Dr. Paul Monroe, Director of the International Institute of Education, Teachers' College.

Mr. Leslie M. Moss, Assistant Secretary of the Foreign Missions Conference of North America.

Mr. George Foster Peabody, Banker and Philanthropist.

Mr. George A. Plimpton, New York Colonization Society.

Mr. John A. Poynton, Trustee of the Carnegie Corporation.

Mr. David A. Robertson, Assistant Director of the American Council on Education.

Dr. Wickliffe Rose, President of the International Education Board.

Professor Johnston Ross, Union Theological Seminary.

Mr. L. A. Roy, Office Secretary of the Phelps-Stokes Fund.

Dr. William F. Russell, Associate Director of the International Institute of Education, Teachers' College.

Dr. William J. Schieffelin, Chairman of the Trustees of Tuskegee Institute.

Mr. James L. Sibley, Educational Adviser of the American Missionary Societies in Liberia.

Dr. Anson Phelps Stokes, President of the Phelps-Stokes Fund.

Mrs. Anson Phelps Stokes.

Miss Helen Phelps Stokes, Trustee of the Phelps-Stokes Fund.

Mr. Fennell P. Turner, Secretary of the Foreign Missions Conference of North America.

Dr. George E. Vincent, President of the Rockefeller Foundation.

Dr. A. L. Warnshuis, Secretary of the International Missionary Council.

Mr. Max Yergan, International Secretary of the Y.M.C.A., assigned to the Union of South Africa.

BIBLIOGRAPHY

Henry Allen Bullock's *A History of Negro Education in the South, From 1619 to the Present* (New York: Praeger, 1970) is a valuable synthesis of the major trends in black educational history in the United States. But to attempt such a vast topic in one volume is by its own nature preclusive. The author's treatment of industrial education is of necessity largely an overview rather than an in-depth analysis. This does not mean that the book does not generate some interesting questions about industrial schooling; it does. However, it generates as many questions as it answers. Much the same can be said of Louis R. Harlan's *Separate and Unequal* (New York: Atheneum, 1968), and his *Booker T. Washington: The Making of a Black Leader, 1856-1901* (New York: Oxford, 1972). In the former, Harlan concentrates on the Southern Education Board and gives important insight into this organization that served as a propaganda agency for Northern philanthropic support to Southern education. However, Harlan devotes little attention to the Rockefeller-sponsored General Education Board through which most so-called philanthropic funds for black education in the South were dispensed. In his noted biography of Booker Washington the focus is on Washington the leader, Washington the statesman, and Washington the black political and business architect, but not on industrial schooling under Washington. Theodore Vincent cites Lerone Bennett on Booker T. Washington and industrial education:

A conservative man, shrewd, hard working and, some
say, devious, Washington essayed a program of con-
ciliation and racial submission. He refused to attack
Jim Crow directly and urged Negroes to subordinate
their political, civil and social strivings to economic
advancement. By implication anyway, he accepted
segregation and concentrated on a program of 'industrial education.'. . ." [Theodore Vincent, *Black Power
and the Garvey Movement* (San Francisco: Ramparts,
1972), p. 54; Lerone Bennett, *Before the Mayflower*
(Chicago: Johnson, 1964), p. 276.]

Vincent adds that Bennett's was a "version of the usual appraisal
of Washington."

Bennett's interpretation is typical of the textbook appraisal
of Washington and of industrial schooling. The same treatment
can be found in John Hope Franklin's classic text on Afro-
American history, *From Slavery to Freedom: A History of
Negro Americans*, 4th ed. (New York: Knopf, 1974). Other
scholars have avoided the vexing issues of industrial education.
In his significant examination of education in the South during
Reconstruction, *Schools for All: The Blacks and Public Education in the South, 1865-1877* (Lexington, Ky.: The University
Press of Kentucky, 1974), William Preston Vaughn carefully
places the industrial schooling issue under the category of "pri-
vately supported institutions" and, therefore, out of the scope
of his study. But Hampton Institute, for example, received
both private and public support as did numerous public institutions. This is given careful documentation in Horace Mann
Bond's classic work, *Negro Education in Alabama: A Study in
Cotton and Steel* (New York: Associated Publishers, 1939),
and in Charles William Dabney's *Universal Education in the
South* (New York: Arno Press, [1936] 1969).

The classic works on the South in general have either paid
only scant attention to the industrial education phenomenon
or have tended to approach it uncritically. C. Vann Woodward
sees the industrial education movement as largely motivated
by noblesse oblige. See Woodward's *Origins of the New South,
1877-1913* (Baton Rouge, La.: Louisiana State University

Press, 1951), pp. 401-444. George Tindall equates industrial education with vocational education. See Tindall's *South Carolina Negroes, 1877-1900* (Baton Rouge, La.: Louisiana State University Press, 1966.

Most recently, James M. McPherson in *The Abolitionist Legacy: From Reconstruction to the NAACP* (Princeton, N.J.: Princeton University Press, 1975) stresses educational opportunity. He contends that "before World War I the northern mission societies founded largely by abolitionists were by far the most important contributors to Negro higher education." (p. 148) Industrial Education, however, was unquestionably the dominant education for blacks by 1915. Moreover, while it is true that most of the missionary teachers were not advocates of black industrial schooling, the contribution to it by them and the missionary societies cannot be denied. McPherson notes that the American Missionary Association helped found Hampton Institute, supplied many of the teachers of industrial schools, and gave financial support to those institutions. This evidence indicates strong ties between missionary and industrial education.

The real issue is not whether the missionary groups contributed more to one than another type of education for blacks. The salient question is: education for what? As Carter G. Woodson concluded in his brilliant analysis of black education in America, the aim of the missionary teachers who came south

> was to transform the Negroes, not to develop them.
> The Freedmen who were to be enlightened were
> given little thought, for the best friends of the race,
> ill-taught themselves, followed the traditional curricula of the times which did not take the Negro
> into consideration except to condemn or pity them.
> [Carter G. Woodson, *The Mis-education of the Negro*
> (1933), p. 17.]

Henry Snyder Enck, in his massive work, "The Burden Borne: Northern White Philanthropy and Southern Black Industrial Education, 1900-1915" (Ph.D. Dissertation, University of Cincinnati, 1970), incorrectly concludes that Northerners who supported industrial education were basically well-meaning individuals harboring no ulterior motives behind their support, but they had some faults. The major fault, according to him, was that the "philanthropists relied too largely on education as an instrument for social change." (p. 533) The most recent, completed study of Hampton Institute is William Hannibal Robinson's "The History of Hampton Institute, 1868-1949" (Ph.D. Dissertation, New York University, 1953), which is a sympathetic chronicle of the school's development.

Recent articles on aspects of industrial schooling are serviceable, although in a limited scope. Allen W. Jones, in "The Role of Tuskegee Institute in the Education of Black Farmers," *Journal of Negro History* 60 (April 1975), notes that Tuskegee Institute served the community by providing it with an agricultural extension program. Booker T. Gardner, in his article, "The Educational Contributions of Booker T. Washington," *Journal of Negro Education* 45 (Fall 1975), summarizes the highlights of Washington's career and the books and articles devoted to him. Henry Enck, in "Black Self-Help in the Progressive Era: The 'Northern Campaigns' of Smaller Southern Black Industrial Schools, 1900-1915," *Journal of Negro History* 61 (January 1976), recounts the efforts of black industrial schools other than Tuskegee and Hampton in obtaining financial support from Northern groups. Interesting articles are those that have gone beyond the traditional treatment and have examined various interrelated facets of the industrial education phenomenon. See Manning Marable, "Booker T. Washington and African Nationalism," *Phylon* 35:4 (December 1974), and Fred H. Matthews, "Robert Park, Congo Reform and Tuskegee: The Molding of a Race Relations Expert, 1905-1913," *Canadian Journal of History: Annales Canadiennes D'Histoire* 8:1 (March 1973).

MANUSCRIPT COLLECTIONS

American Missionary Association Collection. Fisk University (now at Dillard University).
Armstrong Family Papers. Williams College.
Armstrong Collection, Samuel Chapman. Hampton Institute.

Carnegie Papers, Andrew. Library of Congress.
Curry Papers, Jabez Lamar Monroe. Library of Congress.
Frissell Papers, Hollis B. Hampton Institute.
General Education Board Papers. Rockefeller Archives.
Huntington Papers, Collis P. Syracuse University.
International Education Board Collection. Rockefeller Archives.
Ludlow Collection. Hampton Institute, Williams College.
Ludlow, Helen, ed. *Personal Memoirs and Letters of General Samuel Chapman Armstrong: Hawaii, Williams, War, Hampton.* 1894. Hampton Institute.
Ogden Papers, Robert Curtis. Library of Congress.
Records of the Bureau of Refugees, Freedmen, and Abandoned Lands, Virginia, Letters Received. National Archives.
Tuskegee Collection. Tuskegee Institute Archives.
Washington Papers, Booker T. Library of Congress.

ADDRESSES

"Address by Booker T. Washington at Atlanta Exposition, 1895." *Booker T. Washington Papers,* Library of Congress.
"Address by Booker T. Washington at Hampton Institute, 31 January 1909, Some Results of the Armstrong Idea, in Celebration of Founder's Day." *Armstrong Family Papers,* Library of Congress.
"Address by Booker T. Washington at Lincoln University, 26 April 1888: The South as an Opening for a Business Career." *Booker T. Washington Papers,* Library of Congress.
"Address by Booker T. Washington at a Meeting of the New York Congregational Club, 16 January 1893: The Progress of the Negro." *Booker T. Washington Papers,* Library of Congress.
"Address by Booker T. Washington at Raleigh, North Carolina, 30 October 1903." *Booker T. Washington Papers,* Library of Congress.
"Address by Booker T. Washington Before the National Unitarian Association at Saratoga, New York, 26 September 1896." *Booker T. Washington Papers,* Library of Congress.
"Address by C. T. Loram on The Native Affairs Commission, Union of South Africa, on the Occasion of a Dinner Given in his Honour, 4 January 1927." *International Education Board Collection,* Rockefeller Archives.
"Address by Samuel Chapman Armstrong Before the National Education Association, 1872." *Armstrong Family Papers,* Williams College.
"Address by Thomas Jesse Jones at the League of Nations Association Convention, St. Louis, Missouri, 13 January 1933: Liberia and the

League of Nations." *International Education Board Collection*, Rockefeller Archives.

"Founder's Day Address of Robert E. Park at Tuskegee Institute, April 12, 1942." Tuskegee Institute Library.

"Founder's Day Address by Thomas Jesse Jones at Hampton Institute, 1940: Hampton Institute and Dr. Malcolm Maclean." *General Education Board Papers*, Rockefeller Archives.

PUBLISHED REPORTS

Annual Report of the Principal and Officers of Hampton Normal and Agricultural Institute, 1870. Hampton, Va.: Hampton Institute Press, 1870.

———. 1872.

———. 1880-1881.

———. 1883.

Circulars of Information of the Bureau of Education. 1860-1915.

Report of the American Missionary Association (n.d.). Frissell, Hollis B. "Our Responsibility to Undeveloped Races."

Report of the Commission of Education for the Year 1903 (Vol. 1, 1905). Mayo, Amory D. "Services of Doctor Curry in Connection with the Peabody Fund."

Report of Commissioner of Education for the Year 1894-1895 (Vol. 2, 1896). Curry, J.L.M. "Difficulties, Complications, and Limitations Connected with the Education of the Negro."

Report of the Department of the Interior, Bureau of Education, Bulletin no. 23. Aery, Walter. "Hampton Institute." Washington, D.C.: Government Printing Office, 1923.

———. Blodgett, Warren K. "The Agricultural School." 1923.

———. Lyford, Carrie Alberta. "Hampton Institute." 1923.

———. Rowell, Olive B. "Hampton Institute." 1923.

———. Taft, William Howard. "The Influence of Hampton." 1923.

———. Walter, Sarah J. "The Whittier Training School." 1923.

———. Washington, Major Allen W. "Discipline." 1923.

———. Williams, Charles H. "Hampton Institute." 1923.

Report on Educational Needs and Opportunities in Liberia. N.d.

Report of R. R. Taylor upon the Booker Washington Agricultural and Industrial Institute at Kakata, Republic of Liberia. October 1929.

Report of United States Industrial Commission 7 (1900).

Southern Railway Company. "Annual Meeting of Stockholders." *Proceedings.* 1894-1900.

Thirty-seventh Congress, 2nd Session, House of Representatives, Execu-

tive Document No. 85. "Africans in Fort Monroe Military District: A Letter from the Secretary of War." Washington, D.C., 1863.

United States Census. *Ninth-Twelfth Census, 1870-1900: Population.*

United States Senate Committee on Education and Labor. *Testimony Before the Committee to Investigate the Relations Between Capital and Labor* 4. Washington, D.C., 1885.

UNPUBLISHED REPORTS

"Report of the Committee to Inspect Phelps Hall to Booker T. Washington, 22 October 1904." *Booker T. Washington Papers*, Library of Congress.

"Report on Training at Hampton Institute, 4 February 1905." *Armstrong Family Papers*, Williams College.

"Confidential Report by W.T.B. Williams on Tuskegee Institute to the General Education Board, 1906." *General Education Board Papers*, Rockefeller Archives.

"Confidential Report of the Principal of the Tuskegee Normal and Industrial Institute, For Year Ending May 31, 1907." *General Education Board Papers*, Rockefeller Archives.

"Report of Monroe N. Work to the Trustees of the Tuskegee Normal and Industrial Institute, 10 June 1910." *Booker T. Washington Papers*, Library of Congress.

"Special Committee Report to Booker T. Washington, 15 July 1911." *Booker T. Washington Papers*, Library of Congress.

"Report of the Committee to Investigate Flag Raising Incident, 4 January 1912," *Booker T. Washington Papers*. Library of Congress.

"Report on Educational Needs and Opportunities in Liberia." N.d. *International Education Board Collection*, Rockefeller Archives.

MEMOS

"Memo by Booker T. Washington to Himself," 5 March 1904. *General Education Board Papers*, Rockefeller Archives.

"Memo to Anson Phelps Stokes," 21 September 1923. *International Education Board Collection*, Rockefeller Archives.

"Memo from Wickliffe Rose," 8 November 1924. *International Education Board Collection*, Rockefeller Archives.

"Extracts from Memorandum of British Empire Advisory Committee on Education," 1935. *International Education Board Collection*, Rockefeller Archives.

"Confidential memo to members of the New York Colonization Society: Impressions of Liberia—March 31-April 12, 1935." *International Education Board Collection*, Rockefeller Archives.

"Memorandum from Thomas Jesse Jones to Jackson Davis," 26 March 1936. *International Education Board Collection*, Rockefeller Archives.

"Memo to Jackson Davis," 19 August 1936. *International Education Board Collection*, Rockefeller Archives.

MINUTES

"Minutes of the Meeting of the Board of Trustees of the Booker Washington Agricultural and Industrial Institute of Liberia, 22 May 1936." *International Education Board Collection*, Rockefeller Archives.

"Minutes of the Tuskegee Institute Executive Council." 18 May 1898. *Booker T. Washington Papers*, Library of Congress.

————. 27 September 1903.

————. 15 September 1904.

————. 16 September 1910.

————. 1913.

————. 26 March 1914.

PROCEEDINGS

General Education Board, The: An Account of Its Activities 1902-1914.

Proceedings of the Fifth Annual Conference for Education in the South 24 April 1902.

Proceedings of the Fourth Conference for Education in the South 1901, Winston-Salem, N.C.

Proceedings of the Meeting of the Armstrong Association 12 February 1904.

Proceedings of the National Education Association 1872-1915.

Proceedings of the Southern Education Association 1899-1913, Richmond, Va.

Proceedings of the Trustees of the Peabody Fund six volumes 1867-1880, Cambridge, Mass.

Proceedings of the Trustees of the John F. Slater Fund 1899-1909, Baltimore, Md.

NEWSPAPERS

Atlanta Constitution. 1895-1915.

Baltimore Journal. 1905.

Birmingham Age-Herald. 1899-1915.
Birmingham Daily News. 1899-1915.
Birmingham News. 1901-1915.
Boston Evening Transcript. 1902-1904.
East African Standard. 1920-1930.
New York Times. 1903.
Rhodesia Herald. 1922-1925.
Rochester Democrat. 1874-1880.
Southern Workman. 1871-1915.
Virginia Patron. 1876-1880.

PAMPHLETS

Armstrong, Samuel Chapman. *Education For Life.* Hampton, Va.: Hampton Institute Press, n.d.
Armstrong, Samuel Chapman. *Ideas on Education.* Hampton, Va.: Hampton Institute Press, 1908.
Armstrong, Samuel Chapman. *Religious Training.* Hampton, Va.: Hampton Institute Press, n.d.
Catalogue of the Hampton Normal and Agricultural Institute, 1871-72. Hampton, Va.: Hampton Institute Press, 1872.
Concerning Hampton Institute. Hampton, Va.: Hampton Institute Press, n.d.
Everyday Life at Hampton Institute. Hampton, Va.: Hampton Institute Press, n.d.
Some Songs of the Hampton Institute Quartette. Hampton, Va.: Hampton Institute Press, n.d.

JOURNALS AND MAGAZINES

American Missionary Magazine. 1872-1896.
Atlantic Monthly. 1896-1915.
Business Idealism. June 1905.
Commercial and Financial Chronicle 1-41.
Gunton's Magazine 9.
Harper's 49 (1874).
Journal of Social Science. 1880-1904.
Nation 79.
New York World. April 1901.

ARTICLES

Alderman, Edwin A. "Charles Brantley Aycock: An Appreciation." *North Carolina Historical Review* 1 (July 1924): 1-5.

Baldwin, William H. "The Present Problem of Negro Education." *Journal of Social Science* 37 (1899): 1-2.

"Booker Washington Outlines Negro's Duty in Materializing South's Industrial Destiny." *Atlanta Constitution*, 5 February 1911: 11-13.

Clignet, Remi. "Assimilation in African Education." *Journal of Modern African Studies* 8:3 (1970): 425-444.

Davis, Arthur P. "William Roscoe Davis and His Descendants." *Negro History Bulletin* 13 (January 1950): 75-89.

Du Bois, W.E.B. "The Freedmen's Bureau." *Atlantic Monthly* 87 (March 1901): 354-365.

Enck, Henry S. "Black Self-Help in the Progressive Era: The 'Northern Campaigns' of Smaller Southern Black Industrial Schools, 1900-1915." *Journal of Negro History* 61 (January 1976): 73-87.

Gardner, Booker T. "The Educational Contributions of Booker T. Washington." *Journal of Negro Education* 45 (Fall 1975): 502-518.

Grimke, Archibald H. "Why Disfranchisement Is Bad." *Atlantic Monthly* 94 (July 1904): 72-81.

Harlan, Louis R. "Booker T. Washington and the White Man's Burden." *American Historical Review* 81 (January 1966): 441-467.

Jones, Allen W. "The Role of Tuskegee Institute in the Education of Black Farmers." *Journal of Negro History* 60 (April 1975): 257-267.

Marable, Manning. "Booker T. Washington and African Nationalism." *Phylon* 35:4 (December 1974): 398-406.

Matthews, Fred H. "Robert Park, Congo Reform and Tuskegee: The Molding of a Race Relations Expert, 1905-1913." *Canadian Journal of History: Annales Canadiennes D'Histoire* 8, no. 1 (March 1973): 37-65.

Miller, Kelly. "Social Equality." *National Magazine* (February 1905): 1-10.

Morel, E. D. "The Future of Tropical Africa." *Southern Workman*, June 1912: 353-354.

Pierce, P. G. "The Freedmen's Bureau." *Bulletin of State University of Iowa* 74 (1904): 1-25.

Walker, T. C. "Development in the Tidewater Counties of Virginia." *The Annals of The American Academy*, n.d.: 1-39.

Washington, Booker T. "The Awakening of the Negro." *Atlantic Monthly* 78 (1896): 322-328.

Welsch, Herbert. "Samuel Chapman Armstrong." *Education Review* (1893): 105-125.

BOOKS AND THESES

Abels, Jules. *The Rockefeller Billions.* New York: MacMillan, 1965.

Alderman, Edwin A., and Gordon, Armistead C. *J.L.M. Curry: A Biography.* New York: The Macmillan Company, 1911.

Armes, Ethel. *The Story of Coal and Iron in Alabama.* Birmingham, Alabama: Published under the auspices of the Chamber of Commerce, University Press, Cambridge, Mass., 1910.

Armstrong, Mary F., and Ludlow, Helen. *Hampton and Its Students, By Two of Its Teachers.* New York: Doubleday, 1875.

Bennett, Lerone. *Before the Mayflower.* Chicago: Johnson, 1964.

Bond, Horace Mann. *The Education of the Negro in the American Social Order.* New York: Prentice-Hall, 1934.

——. *Negro Education in Alabama: A Study in Cotton and Steel.* New York: Associated Publishers, 1939.

——. *Social and Economic Influences on the Public Education of Negroes in Alabama, 1865-1930.* Washington, D.C.: Associated Pubs., 1939.

Bremner, Robert H. *American Philanthropy.* Chicago: University of Chicago Press, 1960.

Brewer, James H. *The Confederate Negro: Virginia's Craftsmen and Military Laborers, 1861-1865.* Durham, N.C.: Duke University Press, 1969.

Brooks, John Graham. *An American Citizen: The Life of William H. Baldwin.* New York: Houghton Mifflin, 1910.

Bullock, Henry Allen. *A History of Negro Education in the South: From 1619 to the Present.* New York: Praeger, 1917.

Carson, Suzanne. "Samuel Chapman Armstrong: Missionary to the South." Ph.D. Dissertation, Johns Hopkins University, 1952.

Clark, Victor S. *History of Manufacturers in the United States,* Vol. 2. New York: McGraw-Hill, 1929.

Connor, R.D.W., and Poe, Clarence. *The Life and Speeches of Charles Brantley Aycock.* New York: Doubleday, Page and Company, 1912.

Curry, J.L.M. *History of the Peabody Education Fund.* New York: Negro University Press, 1969.

——. *The Southern States of the American Union.* New York: G. P. Putnam, 1894.

Curti, Merle. *The Social Ideas of American Educators.* New York: Scribner's, 1935.

Dabney, Charles William. *Universal Education in the South.* New York: Arno Press, [1936] 1969.

Du Bois, W.E.B. *Autobiography.* New York: International Pubs., 1969.

————. *The World and Africa.* New York: International Publishers, 1946.

Enck, Henry Snyder. "The Burden Borne: Northern White Philanthropy and Southern Black Industrial Education, 1900-1915." Ph.D. Dissertation, University of Cincinnati, 1970.

Engs, Robert. "The Development of Black Culture and Community in the Emancipation Era: Hampton Roads, Virginia, 1861-1870." Ph. D. Dissertation, Yale University, 1972.

Ferguson, Clyde. "The Political and Social Ideas of John D. Rockefeller and Andrew Carnegie." Ph.D. Dissertation, University of Illinois, 1951.

Fleming, Walter L. *Civil War and Reconstruction in Alabama.* New York: Columbia Univ. Press, 1905.

Fox, Stephen R. *The Guardian of Boston.* New York: Atheneum, 1971.

Franklin, John Hope. *From Slavery to Freedom: A History of Negro Americans,* 4th ed. New York: Knopf, 1974.

Fredrickson, George M. *The Black Image in the White Mind: The Debate on Afro-American Character and Destiny, 1817-1914.* New York: Harper and Row, 1971.

Freire, Paulo. *Pedagogy of the Oppressed.* New York: Herder and Herder, 1972. Translated by Myra B. Ramos from the original Portuguese manuscript, 1968.

Garner, James Wilford. *Reconstruction in Mississippi.* New York: The Macmillan Co., 1901.

Graham, Edward K. "A Tender Violence: The Biography of a College." Unpublished Manuscript.

Greene, Lorenzo, and Woodson, Carter G. *The Negro Wage Earner.* Washington, D.C.: Van Rees, 1930.

Greybil, Stanton Becker von. *Letters from Tuskegee: Being the Confessions of a Yankee.* Alabama: Roberts, 1905.

Guild, June Purcell. *Black Laws of Virginia: A Summary of the Legislative Acts of Virginia Concerning Negroes from Earliest Times to the Present.* New York: Negro University Press, 1936.

Harlan, Louis R. *Booker T. Washington: The Making of a Black Leader, 1856-1901.* New York: Oxford University Press, 1972.

————. *Separate and Unequal.* New York: Atheneum, 1968.

Hays, Samuel P. *The Response to Industrialism, 1885-1914.* Chicago: The University of Chicago Press, 1957.

Hofstadter, Richard. *Social Darwinism in American Thought.* Boston: Beacon Press, 1955.

Ingle, Edward. *The Ogden Movement: An Educational Monopoly in the Making.* Baltimore: Manufacturer's Record Pub. Co., 1908.

Jacobson, Julius. *The Negro and the Labor Movement.* New York: Doubleday, 1931.

Jones, Thomas Jesse. *Education in Africa: A Study of West, South, and Equatorial Africa*. London: Edinburg House Press, 1922.

———. *Education in East Africa: A Study of East, Central, and South Africa*. London: Edinburgh House Press, 1925.

Katz, William Loren, ed. *The Negro Problem*. New York: Arno Press, 1969.

King, Kenneth James. *Pan-Africanism and Education: A Study of Race Philanthropy and Education in the Southern States of America and East Africa*. London: Oxford University Press, 1971.

Kirkland, Edward Chase. *Industry Comes of Age*. Chicago: Quadrangle, 1961.

Kolko, Gabriel. *The Triumph of Conservatism*. Chicago: Quadrangle, 1963.

Lewis, L. J. *The Phelps-Stokes Reports on Education in Africa*. London: Oxford University Press, 1962.

Lewis, W. J. "The Educational Speaking of J.L.M. Curry." Ph.D. Dissertation, University of Michigan, Ann Arbor, 1955.

Logan, Rayford W. *The Betrayal of the Negro*. London: Collier Books, 1969.

———. *The Negro in American Life and Thought: The Nadir, 1877-1901*. London: Collier Books, 1965.

Lynch, Hollis R. *Edward Wilmot Blyden*. London: Oxford University Press, 1967.

Malone, Dumas, ed. *Dictionary of American Biography*. New York: Scribner's, 1928-1934.

Mayo, Amory Dwight. *Industrial Education in the South*. Washington, D.C.: Govt Print. Off., 1888.

McFeely, William S. *Yankee Stepfather: General O. O. Howard and the Freedmen*. New York: W. W. Norton and Company, 1970.

McLaughlin, Russell U. *Foreign Investment and Development in Liberia*. New York: Praeger, 1966.

McPherson, James M. *The Abolitionist Legacy: From Reconstruction to the NAACP*. Princeton, N.J.: Princeton University Press, 1975.

Meier, August. *Negro Thought in America, 1880-1915*. Ann Arbor, Mich.: The University of Michigan Press, 1963.

Myrdal, Gunnar. *An American Dilemma: The Negro Problem and Modern Democracy*, Vols. I & II. New York: Harper and Row, 1944.

Nkrumah, Kwame. *Africa Must Unite*. New York: International Publishers, 1963.

Nordhoff, Charles. *The Freedman of South Carolina*. New York: C. T. Evans, 1863.

Ogden, Robert Curtis. *Samuel Chapman Armstrong: A Sketch*. New York: Fleming H. Revell Company, 1894.

Peabody, Francis Greenwood. *Education For Life: The Story of Hampton Institute.* New York: Doubleday, Page and Company, 1918.

Perham, Margery Freda. *Lugard: The Years of Adventure.* London: Collins, 1956.

Pierce, Edward L. *Enfranchisement and Citizenship: Addresses and Papers,* ed. A. W. Stevens. Boston: Roberts Brothers, 1896.

Robinson, William Hannibal. "The History of Hampton Institute, 1868-1949." Ph.D. Dissertation, New York University, 1953.

Rockefeller, John D. *Random Reminiscences of Men and Events.* New York: Doubleday, 1909.

Rodney, Walter. *How Europe Underdeveloped Africa.* Washington, D.C.: Howard University Press, 1974.

Southern Education Board. *Southern Education.* Knoxville, Tenn., 1903.

Spero, Sterling D., and Harris, Abram L. *The Black Worker.* New York: Atheneum, 1968.

Spivey, Donald. "The Role of Industrial Education for the Black South, 1866-1915." M.A. Thesis, University of Illinois, 1972.

———. "White Philanthropy and Black Education." Undergraduate Honors Thesis, University of Illinois, 1971.

Stokes, Anson Phelps. *A Brief Biography of Booker T. Washington.* Hampton, Va.: Hampton Institute Press, 1936.

Tarbell, Ida M. *The History of the Standard Oil Company.* New York: MacMillan, 1904.

———. *The Life of Elbert H. Gary.* New York: Appleton, 1925.

Taylor, Alrutheus Ambush. *The Negro in the Reconstruction of Virginia.* New York: Russell and Russell, [1926] 1969.

Thompson, Clara Mildred. *Reconstruction in Georgia, Economic, Social, Political.* New York: Columbia Univ. Press, 1915.

Thompson, Holland. *The New South.* New Haven, Conn.: Yale Univ. Press, 1919.

Thornbrough, Emma L., ed. *Booker T. Washington.* Englewood Cliffs, N.J.: Prentice-Hall, 1969.

Tindall, George. *South Carolina Negroes, 1877-1900.* Baton Rouge, La.: Louisiana State University Press [1952] 1966.

Vaughn, William Preston. *Schools for All: The Blacks and Public Education in the South, 1865-1877.* Lexington, Ky.: The University Press of Kentucky, 1974.

Vincent, Theodore G. *Black Power and the Garvey Movement.* San Francisco: Ramparts, 1972.

Washington, Booker T. *Character Building.* New York: Doubleday, 1902.

———. *My Larger Education.* New York: Doubleday, Page & Co., 1911.

———. *The Story of My Life.* Atlanta: Nichols, 1900.

———. *Up From Slavery.* New York: Doubleday, 1901.

———. *Working With the Hands.* New York: Doubleday, 1904.

Weinstein, James. *The Corporate Ideal in the Liberal State.* Boston: Beacon Press, 1967.

Willhelm, Sidney. *Who Needs the Negro?* New York: Doubleday, 1971.

Williams, Chancellor. *The Destruction of Black Civilization.* Chicago: Third World Press, 1974.

Woodson, Carter G. *The Mis-education of the Negro.* Washington, D.C.: The Associated Pubs., 1933.

Woodward, C. Vann. *Origins of the New South, 1877-1913.* Baton Rouge, La.: Louisiana State University Press, 1970.

Wright, Richard. *12 Million Black Voices: A Folk History of the Negro in the United States.* New York: Viking Press, 1941.

INDEX

About the Author

DONALD SPIVEY is Assistant Professor of History at Wright State University, Dayton, Ohio. He has contributed articles to such journals as *Social Science Quarterly*, *The New Scholar*, and *Journal of Negro History*.

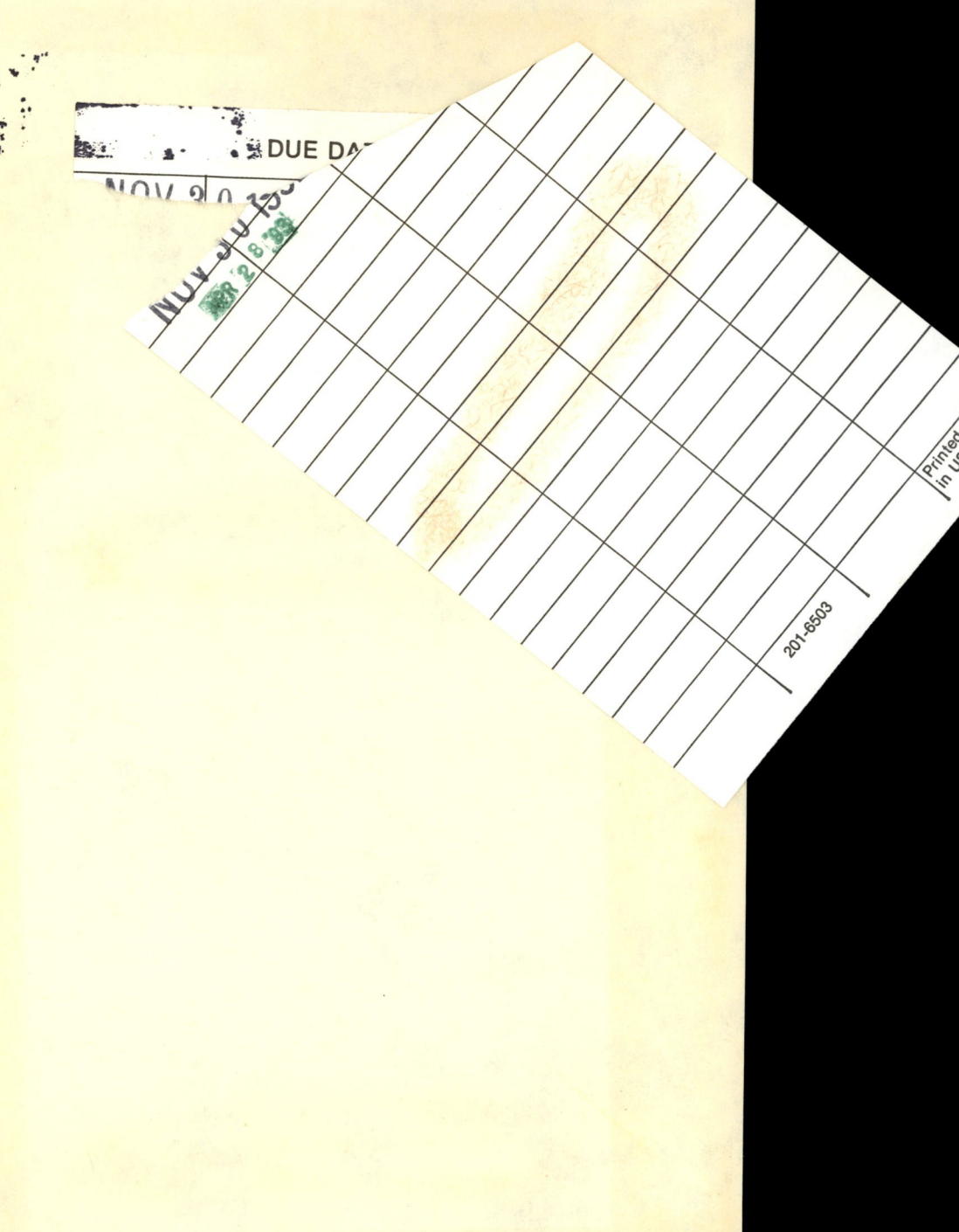